Unto a Land That
I WILL SHOW YOU

*Stories from Fifty Years of
Missionary Life and Ministry in Japan*

AUTOBIOGRAPHY
LEO & PHYLLIS KAYLOR

PRESS

Unto A Land That I Will Show You
by Leo and Phyllis Kaylor

Printed in the United States of America

ISBN 978-1-60034-730-6

Cover: The mountain is majestic Mt. Sakurajima. It is an active volcano across the bay from Kagoshima City, in southern Kyushu, Japan. The Japanese characters at the center of the cover are "Nihon", which means "Japan".

www.xulonpress.com

Praise for
Unto A Land That I Will Show You

Leo and Phyllis Kaylor are two of God's choicest servants in the entire world! In responding to their missionary call to Japan, they began an exciting journey of faith that will both challenge and inspire your heart. This is a tender love story of a couple of ordinary people doing extraordinary things for their Lord.

Carol and I consider it a privilege to know the Kaylors and rejoice in God's faithfulness to them.

Jim Cymbala,
Senior Pastor of the Brooklyn Tabernacle

Carol Cymbala,
*Grammy Award Winning Choir Director of
the Brooklyn Tabernacle Choir
Brooklyn, New York*

Leo Kaylor is one of the most respected, cross-cultural leaders I have known. He is a man of impeccable integrity, with a passion for the lost, persistence in the face of disappointments and delays, and is a man of faith and great vision. He and his wife Phyllis have passed on these great attributes to their own natural children and to their spiritual children. May you reap great benefits in every-way as you read this book.

Frank Damazio
*Senior Pastor of City Bible Church
Portland, Oregon*

It is a great honor and privilege to recommend Leo and Phyllis Kaylor's book to the Body of Christ.

Having been to Japan on a number of occasions, the fruit—the lasting fruit—of the Kaylor's ministry has been seen. It is good fruit, fruit that remains, fruit whose seed is in itself and will go on reproducing itself in strong local churches. Leo and Phyllis Kaylor's book, *Unto A Land That I Will Show You*, tells such a story. It is a must reading of fifty-five plus years of missionary work!

May God's blessing be on the book and all who read it!

Kevin J. Conner
Church Founder, Author, Teacher
Melbourne, Australia

Leo's unwavering faith and commitment has inspired many Japanese believers to enter the ministry. We are proud of his stellar record in Japan as a leader and teacher of upright Christian living.

Leo and Phyllis' six children became successful Bible school graduates and are now serving the family of God. Two of their sons are very effectively pastoring congregations in Japan.

George Evans
Church Planter, Prophet, Evangelist
San Diego, California

In the three decades that my wife Gini and I have known Pastors Leo and Phyllis Kaylor, we can testify to the stellar example their lives are to the Body of Christ. Although *Unto A Land That I Will Show You* is the story of the Kaylors' incredible life journey, it really is a "manual in disguise" on the meaning of true discipleship. With joy I recommend and endorse both the book and the authors. This book should be read by every person who plans on impacting the world for Jesus Christ!

Wendell Smith
Senior Pastor of The City Church
Kirkland, Washington

Pastor Phyllis Kaylor has been a great friend and an incredible example of a godly wife, mother, and minister of the Gospel. The Bible says that the children of the virtuous woman will "rise up and call her blessed." Not only do Phyllis Kaylor's natural children do so, but those of us who are her spiritual children do so as well!

Virginia "Gini" Smith
Senior Pastor of The City Church
Kirkland, Washington

True success in life is fulfilling the will of God. In response to God's profound purpose and calling to give their life to the work of the Lord in Japan, the Kaylors have faithfully and sacrificially served the Lord in our nation for more than fifty years. I am honored to call them my friends and rejoice in the completion of this book.

Masaharu Misaka
Senior Pastor of Kanto Glory Church
Tokyo, Japan

As two young people who had dedicated their lives to the Lord, both Leo and Phyllis Kaylor responded to the call of God and came to our devastated country of Japan soon after World War II. This story that tells of their nearly sixty years of amazing work in Japan will surely go down in the history of mission work in Japan as a masterpiece and one of our national treasures.

Words cannot express the influence they have had on countless people throughout the nation of Japan. I also am one that has been greatly impacted by their life. I honor and respect them with all my heart. It is a privilege to be called their friend and consider it an honor to recommend this book.

Yoshinobu Murakami
Senior Pastor of Charis Church
Osaka, Japan

There is no greater blessing than to have a mentor that one can highly respect. To me, Pastor Leo Kaylor is the greatest example in my life. He has shown me what it is to have a passion for the Word of God, to be a loving husband and excellent father, as well as being a model of Christ-like character in every area of life. I have watched his life for over thirty years and my admiration only increases. I am honored to be able to wholeheartedly endorse this book.

Kunio Nishida
Senior Pastor of Fukuoka Harvest Church
Fukuoka, Japan

It has been a privilege to walk part of this journey with my parents. As I have read and relived some of the blessings and challenges of this book, it has again stirred my faith, as I know it will yours, to believe that God really is in control and He has a great plan and purpose for each of our lives.

Robert Kaylor
Senior Pastor of Ariake Bible Church
Arao, Kumamoto, Japan

I often tell people that the greatest inheritance that has been given to me is my upbringing and the faith of my parents. I am delighted to have the many stories of my parents recorded in this book so it can be handed down to our children and to the generations of their descendants to come. It is also a great joy to share our heritage with the world. I know that everyone reading this book will be inspired and find their lives enriched by it.

Steven Kaylor
Senior Pastor of Hope Church
Tokyo, Japan

Contents

Dedication

We lovingly dedicate this book to our six children—

Robert, Steven, Nathan, Joyce, Joel, and Melodee

who have enriched us with the treasures God placed
within each of them.

Appreciations

For the continual words of encouragement from our children during the writing of this book. They walked with us through many of the experiences that are recorded here.

For the Japanese people who graciously honor us with their acceptance and respect.

For Pastor Dick Iverson, President of Ministers Fellowship International, for the valuable input he has had in our lives and ministry for more than thirty-five years. Pastor Iverson's ministry in Japan has left a great deposit in many Japanese pastors, which continues to produce good fruit.

For Pastor Frank Damazio, Senior Pastor of City Bible Church, Portland, Oregon, for the wisdom and guidance we gleaned from him. Pastor Frank has made numerous trips to Japan to share his deep knowledge of God's Word with Japanese pastors and leaders.

For Barbara Wright, an associate pastor of The City Church in Seattle, Washington. Pastor Barbara came along side of us with her excellent expertise in editing the book.

For our son Joel for working tirelessly, determinedly, and artistically through the details of preparing the book for the printers. His dedicated abilities in the field of publishing were invaluable to us.

For our children Nathan and Joyce for working long hours proofreading the manuscript and offering very helpful suggestions.

For Matthew Barron for his expert work on the layout of the book. When need be, he sacrificed midnight hours to get the task done.

This Book is About:

- The legacy of faith that reaches across the generations.
- The chronicle of two young people who responded to God's call to be missionaries.
- A heartwarming love story that unfolds in Japan.
- Accounts of Japanese lives transformed by the power of Christ.
- The birth and growth of churches in Kyushu Island, Japan.
- Integrating ministry and family life.
- Successfully homeschooling on the mission field.
- A testimony of the privilege and effectiveness of longevity on the mission field.

Japan

An Island Nation

Japan is an island nation in the eastern hemisphere with the Pacific Ocean on its east side. Most of its west side is bordered by the Sea of Japan. Across the Sea of Japan are her closest neighbors: South Korea, North Korea, China, and Russia.

Japan is made up of four large islands: Hokkaido, Honshu, Shikoku and Kyushu. There are also about 3,000 smaller islands. Southern Japan, which includes most of its smaller islands, is bordered on the west by the East China Sea.

Size and Population

Japan's population, as of the year 2000, was about 127 million. This represents approximately one-half the population of the U.S., yet Japan compares in square miles to just less than the state of California. If Japan were placed along side the west coast of the United States, it would stretch from Portland, Oregon, to Baja California.

Geographical Features

Eighty-six percent of Japan's land mass is mountainous. Only thirteen percent of the country can be cultivated. Eighty percent of the population lives on twenty percent of the land.

There are five hundred volcanoes in Japan, some of which continue to be active. Hot springs can be found in all parts of the nation. Hot springs baths are a popular means of relaxation for the Japanese.

There are no large rivers in Japan, since the distance from the mountains to the ocean is short. The fishing industry is one of Japan's main industries. This is done mostly in salt water.

Education

All Japanese children are required to attend school for at least nine years. The literacy rate is considered to be one hundred percent.

Religion

The main religions of Japan are Shintoism and Buddhism. However, more than eighty percent of the Japanese have no personal commitment to either. Nonetheless, most people are passively involved in ancestral worship taught by Buddhism, mingled with Shintoism's belief of many gods. Babies are dedicated at Shinto shrines and funerals are conducted by Buddhist priests. In more recent years, it has become popular to have weddings in Christian chapels performed by ministers of the gospel.

Christianity in Japan

In the past, Christianity has made very slow inroads into Japan. Those committed to Christianity were considered to be little more than one percent of the population. However, more recent statistics show an increasing interest in Christianity, especially among the youth.

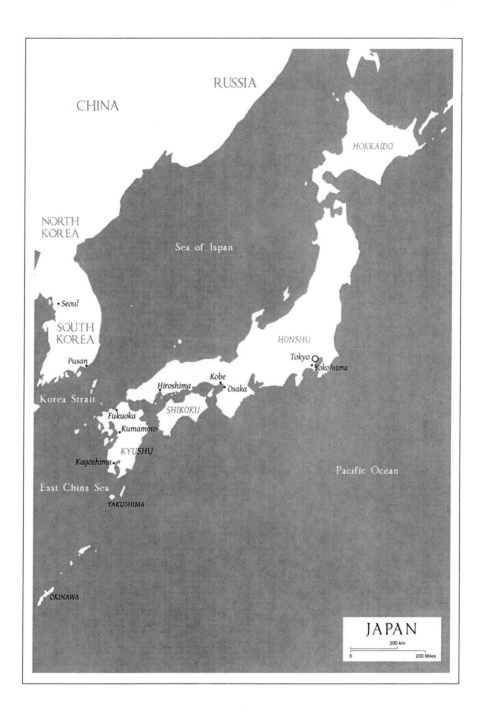

CHINA

RUSSIA

HOKKAIDO

NORTH
KOREA

Sea of Japan

• *Seoul*

SOUTH
KOREA

HONSHU

Tokyo ○
• *Yokohama*

Pusan

Kobe
Hiroshima • *Osaka*

Korea Strait

SHIKOKU

Fukuoka
•*Kumamoto*

KYUSHU

Kagoshima •

Pacific Ocean

East China Sea

YAKUSHIMA

OKINAWA

JAPAN

200 km

0   200 Miles

Foreword

Throughout my years of ministry, I have met hundreds of missionaries, but there are few that I hold in such high respect as Leo and Phyllis Kaylor.

Although I did not know Leo and Phyllis in the first phase of their missionary journey, I was privileged to become closer to them after my first visit to Japan. We have walked together since that time.

In 1973, on behalf of the conference committee, I was invited by Leo to speak at the Japan Pentecostal Ministers Conference. That was one of the landmarks in my life. It was an annual conference that has taken place for many years and has been one of the great heartbeats of God in that nation.

My first observation of Leo and Phyllis was that they had become more Japanese than American. They loved the Japanese people. They not only raised up a great church on the island of Kyushu, but they raised up a godly seed that has been remarkable to behold. All of their children attended Portland Bible College here in Portland, Oregon, and all of them have a deep love and commitment to God, to their parents, and to Japan.

This book is a living testimony of how one couple can make changes in a nation. They have influenced hundreds of pastors from one end of Japan to the other. You will see through their story that life has not always been easy for them. They went through dark times, but never did they lose their love for Japan nor a heart to see Japan changed by the gospel. Even to this day, as you will sense in this book, they are a major influence among the Japanese pastors and continue to believe for a greater move of the Holy Spirit in that great land.

Dick Iverson

President, Ministers Fellowship International
Pastor Emeritus, Bible Temple (now City
Bible Church), Portland, Oregon

Introduction

by Phyllis Kaylor

Many times I had been asked, "Phyllis, why don't you write a book of your life story?" Our children also encouraged me to do so. My response was, "That's a very big task to decide on my own. If God should tell me to write a book, I would give myself unreservedly to write of His gracious Hand upon us. But I wish for a specific word from Him."

In the late fall of 2004, I was meditating through the Psalms in my early morning devotions. That particular morning one of the portions I read was *Psalm 78:4: "We will not hide these truths from our children, but will tell the next generation about the glorious deeds of the Lord. We will tell of His power and the mighty miracles He did"* (NLT). It captivated my heart.

I felt God was clearly saying, "Write the book." I immediately answered, "Yes, Lord. I have received a word from You. To the best of my ability, I will write the book."

Together, Leo and I have endeavored to write this book. Leo wrote his personal story in *Section I. Section II* is my story. In *Section III*, Leo's name is attached to the portions he wrote.

As we recorded incidents of our lives and ministry, we were reminded of Ezra's proclamation, which he repeated several times: *"I felt encouraged because the gracious Hand of the Lord my God was on me" (Ezra 7:28 NLT)*. Whether it was times of blessings or times of trials, God faithfully came along side and stood with us.

Leo and I both were born during the depression years of the 1930s. Leo's family lived in the Ozark Mountains of Arkansas. My family lived in the wheat hills of eastern Washington State. God's loving Hand was upon each of us from our very early childhood.

Leo and I separately answered the call of God to be a missionary to Japan. In the providence of God, we met in Japan and our lives were brought together in marriage.

We tell the story of God's amazing grace through our years of ministry.

We want to leave this legacy for our children, grandchildren, and future generations.

SECTION I

Leo's Story

A Vision from God

It was a cloudy, dreary afternoon that day in late October 1950. I was walking back from a chemistry lab class to my dorm room. It was my third year of pre-medical studies at the University of Arkansas in Fayetteville.

During the summer just a few months before, I had had a fresh encounter with God which ignited my personal faith in the Lord. After that encounter I earnestly desired to know for sure what the will of God was for my life.

A verse from Jeremiah 29 continued to run through my mind:

"...you will seek Me and find Me, when you search for Me with all your heart."

I reached my dorm room, put my books down, and dropped to my knees beside my bed to pray. Suddenly it happened! My eyes were closed, but I could see a verse of Scripture shining on the wall across the room from me. It was as though an overhead projector had flashed these words on the wall:

"Get out of your country, from your kindred, and from your father's house, unto a land that I will show you."

I was stunned! Never had I ever experienced anything like this. I knew immediately the context of this verse was Genesis 12:1. But, just to make sure, I rose to my feet, opened my Bible, and read it aloud. In the vision I saw of the verse projected on the wall, the last four words were all in capital letters and shining brightly:

"...*unto a land that I* WILL SHOW YOU."

I said, "God, is this from You?" And then I said to myself, "Wow! I've been praying to know the will of God for my life, and now God has spoken to me! I don't know any more in detail than I did five minutes ago, but God said that He would show me! I will lay hold of this promise!" A new peace filled my heart to trust God for what He would have for me in the future.

My Christian Heritage

Through the years as I learned more about my ancestral roots, I have been profoundly moved by their faith in God. My ancestors' dedication to God has made it easier for me to follow in their steps. I have deep appreciation for the faith of those who have gone on before me.

Michael Kohler and his two brothers arrived in America from Germany on the ship *Britannia* in 1767. They settled near Philadelphia, Pennsylvania. The German name Kohler was changed to the English spelling of Kaylor after the brothers arrived in America. Later some of Michael's descendants moved to Ohio to homestead. My grandfather Joseph (1845-1922), my father John (1884-1966), and I were all born at that homestead.

Those immigrants from Germany were devout Christians. Some of them, as early settlers, were unable to converse in English and continued to live in their German communities. In 1790 a member of Michael's family purchased a large German Bible for the price of

$10.00. It is thought that the Bible was printed on a German printing press in one of the German communities in America.

That German Bible has been passed down through the Kaylor family for over two hundred years. My father received it in 1937 and passed it on to me in 1961. I, in turn, presented it to our eldest son Robert in 1999. As time goes on, this treasured family heirloom will continue to be passed from father to son.

The German Bible (printed in the U.S. in 1789) purchased by the Kohler family in 1790. The Bible has been passed down through the generations for over two hundred years.

Grandfather Joseph

In 1990 Phyllis and I were visiting my brother Roy and his wife Louise in Houston, Texas. At that time Roy and I were looking through a few of the old family books and records, which he had received from our father. While reminiscing through those old records that day, the following article fell out into our hands.

This article is believed to have been written by my uncle, Dr. Perry B. Fitzwater (1871-1957). Uncle Perry was married to my father's sister Addie. He taught Bible theology at Moody Bible Institute in Chicago, Illinois, for forty-three years. Dr. P. B. Fitzwater was well known and loved by many.

As we began to read, I was captivated by this story of Grandfather Joseph.

In Memory of Joseph Kaylor

Four months have elapsed since the home-going of Father Kaylor (1922). It seems fitting at this distance that a few observations should be recorded concerning his life and death.

He was a large man in physique, mind, and soul. He was born, reared, and lived for 77 years in the same township, and yet his influence now reaches to the other side of the world, especially through the missionary service of his son John. Those who knew him best respected him most. One of his neighbors was heard to say that the best man in the community was gone.

He was a hard working man; frugal and prosperous in business. He had a keen discernment of human nature; sham and unreality did not escape his notice. Though keen in his discernment, he was a man of few words. He lived a clean life; never used tobacco nor intoxicating liquors. As a young man, he learned that Abraham Lincoln did not indulge in these, and this was the incentive which prompted him to abstain from them. In his later years, he looked back with gratitude upon his freedom from these habits.

At a missionary meeting at his home church some months before his death, he started to give the following testimony, which is worth recording for the good it may do for others.

Sometime in his life he was made to feel his obligations to missions, and yet, was unwilling to give freely of his means. He selected from his cattle a blemished steer, sold it, and gave the proceeds to missions. Later his only son John felt the call of God to go as a foreign missionary. It was a great trial to give him up.

At the above-mentioned, he told of what he had done with the blemished steer. He greatly regretted it and said, "I was unwilling to give my best steer, so I was called upon to give my own son to the foreign field." He used this as a concrete example to urge parents not to be unwilling to give their children to the foreign mission field, if God called them. Through his sad failure and bitter experience, he penitentially acknowledged the Hand of God and humbly bowed to His Providence.

Soon after John left last fall (1921) for the second term on the mission field in India, Grandfather felt that he would not live long. He ardently believed in the doctrines of the Church, and some time before his death, he availed himself of the gracious benefits of the precious anointing service according to James 5:14. Then he said, "It doesn't look right for me at my age to ask to live longer, but I would like to live longer for the boys' sake." (His grandsons—Uncle Perry's sons—in whom he took great delight.)

At night in the midst of great suffering, he would say, "Lord, I would like to live a little longer, but not my will but thine be done." Frequently he would repeat the entire Doxology. He said, "I always thought it would be a terrible thing to get ready for death, but, oh, it is not." And as he peered through the thin veil which separated him from the eternal world, he evidenced the realization of the glory of that world.

The night before his death he was heard praying for the missionaries in China, India, Japan, and Africa. Then he begged to be separated from his body and finally said, "Tomorrow the separation will take place." So the following day his spirit took its departure to be with the Lord.

A few days before his death he gave full instructions as to his business, signed checks for bills due, and told how Mother should be cared for. Two ineffaceable impressions were left upon my mind as I watched by his bedside those hours:

1. The reality of the Christian faith. The hour and article of death put to the test the Christian's faith. Father Kaylor had such a real hold upon Christ that with calmness and courage he faced death, made arrangements for his business and his funeral. He selected the pallbearers and the officiating minister. It is highly important that our relationship to Christ be such while we live that death will not be a leap into the dark, but a passing through the door to the freedom and joy of the future life.

2. The reality of the human personality apart from the body. Father Kaylor was conscious to the last. The night before his departure he prayed for the body to be separated from him and said that on the morrow the separation would take place. A few hours before the separation he got out of the bed and helped push the bed to the position he desired it.

To linger at the bedside of a dying Christian will teach one more real philosophy and psychology than a course in a modern university. It puts the lie to all the speculation of the materialistic philosophy.

Roy's Memories

After Roy and I together read this outstanding article about our Grandfather Joseph, Roy remembered comments a cousin had made to him some years before. It was concerning the glorious experience Grandfather Joseph had as he was being released from his body. Roy wrote this postscript:

My cousin, then age 21 or 22, was at Grandfather's bedside just before he was separated. He told me the following: "Suddenly the weak body came alive. He sat up and his eyes sparkled. His hands were raised and his mouth opened in amazement. His words were, 'It's so wonderful!' as he looked into heaven for a moment. Then his arms fell and he collapsed on his pillow. His eyes closed and he was gone."

I was moved to tears that day as Roy and I read this story of our Grandfather Joseph.

I deeply sensed that his prayers for the missionaries many years previously had helped prepare a smooth path for my going to Japan as a missionary.

Grandfather Joseph and Grandmother Nancy (seated). Daddy, John I. Kaylor, (standing) just before he left for India for his second missionary term. Addie, Daddy's sister, at right. She was wife of P. B. Fitzwater (Uncle Perry), a theology professor at Moody Bible Institute for forty-three years.

Boyhood Days

I was born in Ohio in 1931 on the old family homestead. My parents John and Ina Kaylor had returned to the States in 1929, after fifteen years of missionary work in India. Although they were not able to go back to India again, our home life was always filled with a wonderful missionary spirit of consecration and sacrifice.

When I was six years old, my parents moved our family from Ohio to Arkansas. They had a two-fold purpose for this move. There was a Christian school in Sulphur Springs, Arkansas where they wanted to enroll my brother Roy, my sister Eilene, and me. Also, the Ozark mountain range in Arkansas had many rural communities. My parents wanted to minister the gospel to those in spiritual need.

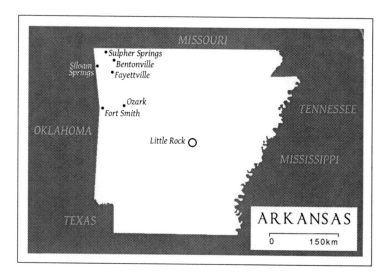

I grew up in the small town of Sulphur Springs. It boasted of a population of 936 and was part of the beautiful hill country in the Ozark Mountains. Sulphur Springs got its name from the several sulphur water wells in town. In fact, our own home had a sulphur water well. To someone unaccustomed to the sulphur water, at first it smelled strongly like rotten eggs. But to us it was cool, clear, delicious, drinking water.

Our family attended church regularly, and I believed in Jesus from the time I was a small child. When I was eleven or twelve years old, with the encouragement and help from my mother, I memorized about one hundred Bible verses.

The memorization course was called, *"The Plan of Salvation from Beginning to End."* For my accomplishment I received a new Bible which I continued to use and prize for many years. The Bible verses I memorized as a child have been a powerful influence to me throughout my life.

Very close to our home was a large school complex. For several years in the early 1940s, the Wycliffe Bible Translators used those facilities for their Summer School of Linguistics. Missionaries were trained to put unwritten languages into writing. This enabled them to then translate the Bible into those languages.

Our family in 1934: Daddy and Mama (John and Ina Kaylor)
with me (3), Eilene (7), and Roy (10)

Because of the personal interest my parents had in missions, they often invited missionaries to our home for fellowship. The presence of many missionaries in our home made a deep impression upon my young mind about becoming a missionary.

High School and University Days

In the rural area in Arkansas where I grew up, we didn't have electricity in our home until I was in high school. My mother cooked on a wood stove. Our house was warmed with a wood heating stove in the winter. We used kerosene lamps for light. I can remember very vividly seeing my father reading his Bible early in the morning as he sat beside the small kerosene lamp.

During my high school years, each morning I would always stop for a few minutes before leaving home and my mother would pray for me. She would pray that God would bless me and protect me from harm and evil. I know that God heard and answered those prayers.

In high school I enjoyed such subjects as Chemistry, Physics, and Biology. In view of this, someone suggested that perhaps I should become a doctor. I personally thought that some day I would be a missionary. Perhaps I could become a medical missionary in some needy country like India or Africa.

With this in mind, after graduating from high school in 1948, I entered the University of Arkansas in Fayetteville and enrolled in the pre-medical course. My major subject was Zoology; I especially enjoyed the lab classes.

During my first year, we dissected and learned all the parts of a large, twelve-inch earthworm. The second year it was a frog; and the third year, a cat. Each was kept preserved in formaldehyde solution. Every time we worked on these specimens to learn their parts, the formaldehyde fumes would burn our eyes and nostrils.

We studied the cat for an entire semester and learned all the muscles of the body, the bones, the circular, respiratory, and nervous systems. We were told that when we got into medical school, we would have a cadaver (human body) to dissect and study. However, I never reached medical school.

After the end of my second year of university, I had a wonderful encounter with Christ. Although I had believed in Jesus from my childhood, I still lacked the deep joy of the assurance of salvation. One night at the close of a Youth for Christ rally, the Holy Spirit spoke very clearly to my heart.

During the altar call, a pastor tapped me on the shoulder and asked about my assurance of salvation. He led me through many of the very same verses I had memorized as a child. When the Bible says, *"All have sinned and fall short of the glory of God,"* that night I knew that I had sinned and come short of the glory of God!

When the Bible says, *"The wages of sin is death,"* that night I knew I was under the condemnation of sin and death. When the Bible says, *"Christ died for our sins,"* that night I knew that Christ died for my sins.

Down at the altar, I prayed and confessed my sin. Jesus said, *"He who hears My word and believes in Him who sent Me has everlasting life, and shall not come into judgment, but has passed from death into life."* That night my faith in Jesus was activated upon the Word of God, and I experienced the great joy of the assurance of salvation that I had never known before.

Following this experience I returned to the university for my third year. My Christian life became alive and vibrant. I began earnestly seeking to know God's definite will for my life. Did God really want me to become a doctor or a medical missionary in some foreign country? If not, then what was God's plan for me?

It was in the fall of that year that I experienced the vision I mentioned earlier when God had spoken to me from *Genesis 12:1*,

"...unto a land that I WILL SHOW YOU." I knew that God would definitely lead me in every detail of His will when the right time came.

The Time Sheet

A short time after I had the renewed experience of God in my life, I felt God's finger on things that He wasn't pleased with.

I was working part-time in the student cafeteria to help meet my school expenses.

I was responsible to keep a record of the hours I worked each day. Shamefully, I began writing down more time than I actually had worked. This boosted my pay check a little each month. After all, didn't I need all the money I could get to meet my school bills?

One day the Holy Spirit convicted me about this dishonesty. I knew that I must never again be dishonest about reporting how many hours I worked. However, that was not the end of the matter. Every time I would kneel to pray, all I could see was my past time-sheets with the dishonest hours written on them. I knew my prayers were not reaching God and I had no peace in my heart.

I knew that I must confess what I had done and pay back all the extra money I had received dishonestly. I calculated how much this would be and determined to return each pay check until that amount was paid back in full. I had no idea how the rest of my needs would then be met. However, God worked in a miraculous way. Once again peace returned to my heart.

This short saying had a powerful impact upon me:

> *"Only one life, 'twill soon be past;*
> *Only what's done for Christ will last."*

For a long time, I had a great desire to be able to lead people to Christ. However, when I tried to witness to others of Christ's salvation, I always ended in failure and confusion.

It was during this time I heard of a soul winning training school in Los Angeles, California. Christians were trained to be effective in witnessing for Christ. At the end of my third year of university, God led me in a definite way to enroll in this three-month course. That was June 1951.

At this training school, I found myself in a class with nearly one hundred others. We were all from different church backgrounds and of various ages. Some were young, like myself; others were moms and dads; and still others were grandmas and grandpas. All had the same desire to become more effective witnesses to win others to Christ.

At the close of that soul winning training course in August, I was once again faced with making a decision for the next step in my life. Should I return to the university to continue with my pre-med studies, or did God have something else for me?

General MacArthur Calls for Missionaries

In January 1946, just a few months after World War II ended, General Douglas MacArthur made an appeal for one thousand missionaries to come to Japan immediately.

General MacArthur, as the Supreme Commander of the Far East, was at that time in a position to decree that Christianity would be the official religion of Japan, thus replacing Shintoism as the national religion. I understand that, in fact, there were strong voices urging him to make such a decree.

General MacArthur had the spiritual understanding to know that Christianity cannot be forced upon a people by official edict, but rather must be accepted by personal choice. Therefore, he called upon the American church to send one thousand missionaries immediately.

However, in 1946 there were very few young men or women prepared to go to Japan as missionaries. It was five or six years before missionaries finally started moving in that direction. And then, between 1950 and 1955, the total number of missionaries going to Japan escalated to some five thousand.

My Call to Japan

The mission's department of the training school I attended in Los Angeles had responded to General MacArthur's appeal for missionaries. They had set a goal as a mission to send one hundred missionaries to Japan. This was 1951.

The mission policy was that each missionary was responsible for all of his or her own financial needs. That was the only workable way they could set the high goal of one hundred missionaries to go out over a short period of time. The mission would act as home base for the missionaries.

Their challenge was: "The door is wide open! The need is great! Go now! Whether young or old, you can have a part in taking the gospel to Japan."

Yes, this was indeed, a *divine moment of opportunity!*

In August, at the close of that summer training course, three days of prayer and fasting were set aside for all who were seeking God's direction in their lives. I was one of them.

The three days of prayer and fasting started Monday morning. Sunday night I simply prayed that God would somehow speak to me in the next three days. I then went to bed. Very early the next morning, I was awakened with the words of a Japanese chorus, which I had learned a few weeks earlier, throbbing through my mind. I woke up with a start and thought, "What does this mean?" Then I remembered, "Oh yes, I am seeking to know God's will for my life. I wonder if God is trying to say something to me about going to Japan."

As each day of prayer and fasting passed, God continued to speak to me from various Scriptures, such as:

> *"From the rising of the sun, even to its going down,*
> *My name shall be great among the Gentiles" (Malachi 1:11).*

I knew that "The Land of the Rising Sun" was Japan, but I still had doubts in my heart about God's will for me. The morning of the third day, I prayed that God would confirm His will to me.

Suddenly, I saw another vision. I saw myself in a large, oval room which had many doors going out from it. All of those doors were closed except the one directly in front of me and it was wide open. Over the top of this door was written, JAPAN. I said, "Yes, Lord! I will go through this door!"

The mission's department accepted me as one of their missionaries, and I began to prepare for going to Japan. My departure date was set for December 5, 1951. I had about three months to prepare. I returned to Arkansas to be with my parents for about six weeks.

The Draft Board

The Korean Conflict, which lasted from 1950 to 1953, was at its height, and many young men were being drafted into the army. Because I had not returned to the university for my senior year, I became a university dropout. My draft board promptly re-classified me as 1-A. This meant I was susceptible to being drafted at any time. I was not free to leave the country.

I contacted my draft board and requested a deferment for missionary work in Japan.

They said I would need credentials to show that I was an ordained minister of the gospel. I finally worked through all of their requirements. In the end they said to me, "You can probably do more good in Japan as a missionary than being a soldier in Korea!"

Again I realized that God had graciously led me through that open door into ministry in Japan.

With Mama, Daddy, and my sister Eilene just before I left for California, and then on to Japan

Farewell to My Parents

The weeks I spent with my parents in Arkansas quickly came to an end. It was time for me to say farewell. The Greyhound Bus ride would take three days to reach California. From there I would go by a freighter to Japan.

My father and mother, along with others, came to the bus depot to see me off. I boarded the bus to leave. I looked out the window and saw my mother waving her handkerchief. Her face was smiling brightly as she was saying, "Good-bye!"

It was several years later when we were back in the states for our first furlough that others told me "the rest of the story." My mother had written to family members that after I was out of sight, she had wept. But she rejoiced that I did not have to see her tears. My mother had said, "I wanted Leo to know that I, as his mother, was so very happy to see my son taking the gospel to the mission field."

Little did I know that would be the last time I would see my mother. Only six months after I arrived in Japan, I received word that she had passed away. The image of her smiling face on that last day of parting remains vividly imprinted on my mind.

My parents, John and Ina Kaylor, 1951

First Days in Japan

I was a member of a team of five missionaries and two children going to Japan. We boarded a Norwegian freighter on December 5, 1951, and sailed out of the Long Beach, California Harbor. At that time, traveling by plane was very expensive.

By traveling on a freighter, we had first class accommodations for a very reasonable price. Our staterooms were all on the first deck, and we ate our meals with the captain and the officers of the ship. Our trip took eighteen days to cross the Pacific Ocean. We arrived in Japan at the Port of Kobe on December 23, just two days before Christmas.

After checking all of our freight through customs and finishing the procedure for entering the country, we left Kobe by train to travel to Kyushu. Kyushu is the southernmost of Japan's four main islands. Apart from our own mission group, there were few missionaries on Kyushu Island.

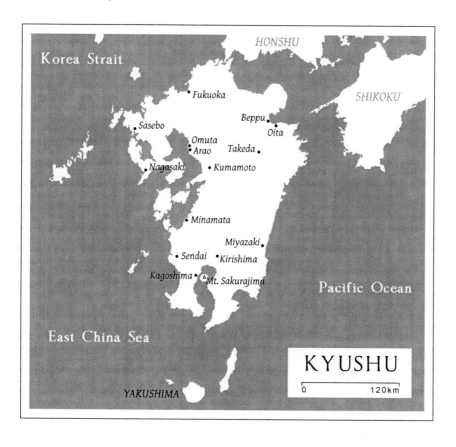

The vision of our mission was to place missionaries in all the major cities around the island. The number of missionaries in our mission at that time was about thirty or forty. As more missionaries continued to arrive, our number eventually reached seventy or eighty.

I was directed to go to Miyazaki to work with another single, young man who had arrived in Japan a few months earlier. He was supposed to meet me when I arrived at the train station, but he was not there. I had his address and found my way to his apartment, which consisted of two upstairs rooms. The landlord and his family lived downstairs.

It was December 29 when I reached Miyazaki. The missionary had left a letter saying he was away to a year-end convention. He said that he would be back in a few days. I was all alone. I didn't know anyone and I only knew a few words of the Japanese language.

I went to the store to buy some things to eat. I had exchanged my dollars to Japanese yen while still in Kobe. At the small roadside store, I picked out some bread, eggs, apples, and a few canned food items. I didn't understand what was said, so I would just hold out my money and the shop owner would take the amount she needed.

On New Year's Day, the landlord's daughter was sent to my room. The household wanted to extend their kindnesses to me by offering me a drink of the traditional New Year's wine. I appreciated their kindness I was offered, but as politely as possible, I turned it down.

On January 2 the missionary with whom I was to work returned. He was twenty-seven years of age; I was twenty. He said he was leaving immediately for another convention in Nobeoka, so I went along with him. At Nobeoka we met with other missionaries and Japanese Christians. That was very refreshing, especially after the lonely days I had just spent by myself.

After the convention the two of us returned to Miyazaki and made plans for our work of evangelizing. We would spend each morning studying the Japanese language. Then each afternoon we would go out on the streets, pass out tracts, and witness to as many people as we could. In those days we, as Americans and foreigners, attracted a lot of attention wherever we went. Many people, especially school students, would gather around us on the street to talk with us.

I could understand very little that people would ask me or say to me. However, I had memorized a few sentences in Japanese about salvation, and I would go through a simple plan of salvation with all who would listen. I had also memorized several verses of Scripture which I would share with them.

A Cablegram from Home

One day in June 1952, I received a cablegram from home saying my mother had passed away. It had been several weeks since I had heard from home, and I was not aware that my mother had been sick and in the hospital. Her passing came as a real shock.

At that time my parents were teaching in a Bible school in Ozark, Arkansas. My mother had suffered for many years with painful arthritis in her knees. Nevertheless, she had always remained active in teaching and was loved by all who knew her. I know that she had prayed earnestly for me, especially during my high school and university years when I was facing major decisions in my life. I believe she had literally prayed me out to the mission field and had rejoiced when I left for Japan.

My mother had had an intense hunger in her heart to know the Lord in a more intimate way. That hunger was satisfied as she entered the Presence of the Lord.

Hot and Humid Summer Days

In June we experienced our first rainy season in Japan. The rainy season is just that—it rains for weeks on end. It lasts through June and into July, creating dampness everywhere. Mold has a heyday! Gradually the rainy season gives way to the extremely hot and humid summer days of July and August.

Some of our missionaries had found a mountain resort high up in the Kirishima Mountains of southern Kyushu. There were a number of newly built bungalows at a campsite. The cooler temperatures made for a very inviting location.

Our mission director sent a call out for all of our missionaries to gather together at the campsite in the Kirishima Mountains. During the month of August, we would all study the Japanese language in the cooler temperatures of Kirishima.

Some fifty missionaries, including those who had just recently arrived in Japan, gathered and camped in the bungalows for a month. We all gave ourselves to diligent language study during the morning hours. The afternoons were a bit more relaxing for everyone.

Meeting a New Friend

Phyllis Poe was one of the newly arrived missionaries. She attracted my attention. One afternoon I asked her, "Would you like to go for a walk with me?" She seemed pleased to respond "Yes," and we walked on some of those lovely, mountain paths together. I found her to be a friend with whom I could openly share my thoughts. Our wonderful afternoon walks continued, and I eagerly looked forward to our times together.

By the end of August, it was time for all of the missionaries to return to their separate mission stations. I was planning to move to Sendai in the southern end of Kyushu to begin a new pioneer work. Phyllis would return to her assignment in Oita in the northeast part of the island.

Before we all scattered, I asked Phyllis another question, "Would you write back to me if I wrote you a letter once in a while?" She said she would be most happy to do so! I was thrilled! I began writing to Phyllis once each week telling her all about my witnessing activities. She would answer, telling everything about what she was doing. I eagerly waited for her letter each week.

Pioneering in Sendai

One morning soon after moving to Sendai, I was reading my Bible and praying. I read John 20:21: *"As my Father hath sent me, even so send I you."* The pronunciation of "Sendai" sounds like, "send I." I felt that the Lord was saying, "Yes, I have sent you to the right place at the right time!"

As 1952 drew to a close, we missionaries in the southern part of Kyushu Island began to plan and prepare for a New Year's conference for all of the people who were gathering in our churches. We would all come together in the missionaries' house in Kagoshima for the first three days of the New Year of 1953.

New Year's Conference

In one of my letters to Phyllis, I asked her another question, "Would you like to come and attend the New Year's conference with me?" Her response was that she would be most happy to do so. Again, I was thrilled!

The conference ended and everyone returned to their homes. Phyllis and I remained for two days with the two missionary ladies with whom we were staying. We wanted to have a little time for ourselves. We enjoyed those two wonderful days. I wanted to ask Phyllis another question—this time the *big one*, "Will you be my wife?" But how could I know for sure if this were really the will of God for us?

We were planning to return to our separate locations on Sunday. Very early that morning, sometime before it was even dawn, I was praying in my heart to know the will of God concerning this matter. I sensed that I was seeing all the way up into heaven. I saw the Lord looking down upon me and smiling! It was then that I knew that, "Yes, this is God's will for us!"

Phyllis and I boarded the crowded train at ten o'clock that morning. I had just an hour and a half before I would have to say, "Good-bye," and get off the train at Sendai. She would go on to her own place of ministry. On that extremely crowded train, I mustered my courage and asked *the question!* Again, she said, "Yes! It would be a privilege for me to be your wife!" We were both thrilled!

Later we set the date for our wedding for May 27, 1953. Since then we have continually experienced God's smile upon us through all of our years together.

SECTION II

Phyllis' Story

Call to Japan

It was October 1951. I was standing with head bowed at the close of a Sunday afternoon service. A heart-stirring challenge of the need for missionaries to go to Japan had been given. "All who would be willing to go to Japan if God should call you...please stand." I stood along with a number of others who had also responded to the challenge.

Ever since I was very young, missionaries' stories had tugged at my heart. Often during my childhood and teen years, I had responded to challenges to be a missionary. Those challenges were always stated the same, "Would you be willing to go as a missionary if God should call you?" The "if" made it easy to respond to such challenges.

As I stood there that day in October 1951, God began digging deeply into my heart. I opened my heart with all sincerity. "O God, in the past I've responded to many challenges to be a missionary. I know just standing here today will get me no place. Therefore, O God, I'm going to make my commitment more definite. I'm going to start making plans to go to Japan unless you close the door." It was a sincere cry from my heart. The gracious Hand of the Lord touched me. Peace filled my being.

That happened at a soul winning training school in Los Angeles, California. I was attending the fall session of a three-month intensive training course on the hows of winning people to Christ. I was nineteen. After graduating from high school, I had attended Prairie Bible Institute in Canada for two years. Now here I was, yearning to serve God and embarking on plans to go to Japan as a missionary.

The soul winning training course ended in December and I returned home. Home was about a thirty-hour bus journey back to Washington State. My family had lived in the Yakima Valley since I was eleven. Home was now near the small community of Prosser.

Home was a wonderful place for me. Family warmth always penetrated our lives. I knew Daddy and Mama would encourage me in my decision to go to Japan as a missionary. But that journey home became a nightmare I would never forget.

Christian Heritage

I had the privilege of a great Christian heritage. My wonderful parents, Everett and Viola Poe, and my grandparents were all devout Christians. Daddy's parents were William and Nellie Poe. Edward and Ethel Summers were Mama's parents. Both families were homesteaders near the small town of Hay in the wheat hills of Washington State.

Children and grandchildren all referred to Daddy's parents as "Dad and Ma." Mama's parents were known as "Papa and Grandma" to all the grandchildren.

My appreciation of my parents' and grandparents' devotion to God has grown through the years. Because of their faithful walk with God, my pathway to walk in the same devotion was made easier.

Dad, my grandfather, had only gone to school through the fourth grade. Hearing him read his Bible is etched deeply in my

Dad and Ma (William and Nellie Poe). This picture represents some of my earliest memories of my grandparents.

memory. My dear grandfather would always run a well-weathered finger along the page where he was reading and softly mumble the words—precious memories I will never forget.

But it hadn't always been that way for Dad and Ma. Neither of them grew up knowing anything about God.

Papa and Grandma (Edward and Ethel Summers). They were just home from church and Papa still had his Bible in his hand.

About 1916 a traveling evangelist came to the small community of Hay. He set up his tent and had meetings every night for a period of time. My grandmother, Ma, attended the meetings and was wonderfully saved. She was so completely changed, it brought a deep conviction on my grandfather.

The following year the evangelist came again with his one-pole tent that would seat thirty to forty people. Here is what Daddy wrote concerning my grandfather's conversion:

> *I was then fifteen years old. We were living on a wheat ranch about three and a half miles from Hay. My dad was*

hired as foreman of the ranch, and my mother was the cook for the workers.

One Sunday my mother asked my dad if he would take her to the tent that evening so she could be in the service. My father readily consented to take her. He hitched one of the ranch horses to a light carriage, and together they went to the tent meeting.

That night when the invitation was given for those to come forward that wanted to be saved, my dad went up and knelt at the altar.

Dad and Ma didn't get home until late that night. When we kids and the ranch hands saw my dad the next morning, he was a new creation—old things had passed away and all things had become new. He threw his pipe and cigars away. I never knew him to ever smoke again or swear again for the rest of his life.

That morning he asked a blessing at the breakfast table. This was the first time it had ever been done in our home. It made a deep impression on me.

My father's completeness in surrendering his life to God had a profound effect upon me as a boy of fifteen.

Daddy's Conversion

When my daddy, Everett Poe, was about seventeen, he left home to find work. Most of his jobs were working for wheat farmers. About a year later, he found work near Pendleton, Oregon. It was now 1920 and Daddy was eighteen.

A traveling evangelist came to Pendleton and pitched his tent for nightly meetings. For tent meetings, when sawdust was available, it was used to cover the bare ground. This made a clean and fragrant "floor".

One night a group of young men was looking for some excitement. They thought it would be fun to go to the tent and see what was going on. Daddy was among them. Standing on the outside of the tent, the boys found some small holes in the canvas. Peering through those holes gave them a good view of what was going on inside. Most of the boys were ridiculing and heckling.

The next night they all decided to go again. Daddy had been very impacted by what he observed through the small hole the previous night. He told his friends he was going inside. The rest of the boys were content to peer through the small holes and continue their heckling.

Daddy was gloriously saved that night. The following night he went to the tent meeting again and experienced a tremendous baptism of the Holy Spirit. As Daddy told it, he lay for several hours on the sawdust-covered ground with God's glorious Presence coming in waves upon him.

My Birth

Daddy and Mama were married in 1928. They set up their home in a small, old farmhouse about a mile up the road from the township of Hay. Back in the 1930s, the town boasted of a population of about 500. Many were wheat farmers.

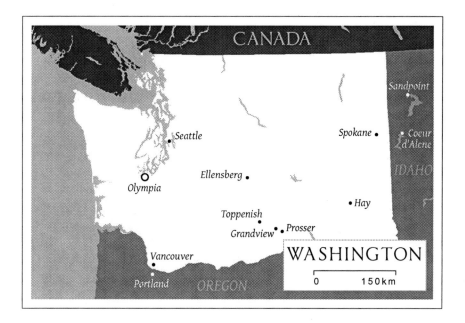

Daddy and Mama's wedding picture (1928)

The house where I was born (Hay, Washington)

Zella (5), me (3), Paul (4)

On March 19, 1932, in that old farmhouse, Daddy and Mama welcomed me into the family.

I was their third child. My sister Zella, two years old, and brother Paul, one, were part of the welcoming party. Mama now had three babies in diapers with only a washboard for doing all the family laundry.

Our closest neighbors were Papa and Grandma, who were wheat farmers. They lived about a quarter of a walking mile over the hills from us.

A Brush with Death

Daddy always had a cow that provided us with all the milk and butter we could use. Mama raised a few chickens that supplied us with eggs, while the garden provided our vegetables. Occasionally the Watkins man would work his way over the countryside peddling his products. Mama would trade eggs for something she needed from his wares.

One day Mama sent Zella and Paul to the barn to get some wheat from the granary to feed her chickens. The barn was a little distance from the house. Mama had already carefully instructed Zella and Paul (now about five and four) that the sacks of wheat on the left of the narrow granary were for feed. The sacks on the right were Papa's seed-wheat for his next year's wheat crop.

The seed-wheat had been treated with a poison that deterred rats and mice from eating it. It was simply called "treated wheat." The mice would chew little holes in the sacks which allowed small amounts of the treated wheat to trickle onto the cement floor. "Don't touch the treated wheat," Mama again carefully instructed Zella and Paul. They were capable of carrying out Mama's charge. I, at three, was just following along. I have no memory of this incident. It was told to me.

I must have seen a bit of the treated wheat on the floor and put some in my mouth.

We children would sometimes chew bits of wheat in this way, especially if we happened to be a little hungry.

Before long I became deathly ill and lapsed into convulsions. Mama said at one point I turned blue and breath seemed to be gone. She frantically laid me on the kitchen table, dashed outside, and screamed to Daddy who was working nearby, *"Phyllis is dying!"*

Daddy rushed into the kitchen, threw his hands heavenward, and in desperation cried out to God, *"Heal her, O God, and we will give her to You for all of the days of her life!"* The gracious Hand of the Lord touched me. The clutches of death released their grip and I was instantly healed. God accepted the sacrifice Daddy had laid on the altar.

Days of the Great Depression

Zella, Paul, and I were born in the days of the Great Depression. Many families in our community learned to make do with little. Daddy and Mama were poor—poor in worldly goods, but not in spirit. I never remember Daddy and Mama complaining about things they didn't have. We kids knew we were poor, but that didn't matter much. We also knew we were a happy family.

Sometimes Daddy and Mama would take their guns to go hunting for pheasants or rabbits in the surrounding hills. They would always take the three of us along with strict orders to follow behind them in single file. We usually returned home with something for supper.

Other times we would all climb into Daddy's old truck and go to the Snake River about eight miles away. Daddy and Mama loved to fish. Those fishing trips not only provided supper, they were also great fun. Daddy and Mama kept a watchful eye out for rattlesnakes that were not uncommon in the dry and rocky areas along the river. We had to walk through those areas to get to the place that was usually our fishing spot.

We three children didn't have fishing poles in those days. Before Daddy would get his own fishing gear ready, he would always go to the nearest willow tree and cut three small limbs. He'd rig each of them with a line, a cork, a small lead weight, and a small hook. It was perfect gear for catching perch and blue gill that were abundant in the shallow sloughs along the river. Supper that night would be a delicious fish fry. We ate whatever we caught, even the bony squaw fish and carp. It was all good food to us.

It's not how much we have,
but how much we enjoy
that makes happiness.

—Spurgeon

Making do in Hard Times

Zella, Paul, and I learned at an early age how to earn a few pennies. I was probably six or seven when we learned from Daddy the value of metals. Each of us became mindful of things like brass, copper, zinc, and aluminum. No matter how small the piece, it became of value to us. After a time Daddy would take our small collections to town to sell them to the man who bought scrap metal. We usually profited only a few pennies, but those were valuable pennies to us.

We also learned that bones were salable. One day the three of us each got a gunnysack and told Mama we were going into the hills to look for bones. Our little dog Snapper went along on the excursion. The hills around us were good hunting grounds for bones of many kinds. The hills were full of rabbits, coyote, badgers, skunks, and a few porcupine.

To our great delight that day, we came upon the carcass of a cow. But it needed considerably more time before the bones would be "bone dry." Since we couldn't carry our find home that day, Paul quickly spoke up, "I dubs the head bone." And from there we each laid claim to certain parts of the partially dried carcass. But the process of time to the "bone dry" stage turned out to be too long. Our enthusiasm over our find faded away. We never did go back to possess our claims of the cow's skeleton.

Another source of income in the summertime for us children was swatting flies. That source was abundant. Our wages were a penny a hundred. Every afternoon we would get an old can, put a bit of water in the bottom as Mama had instructed, and start in on the fly population in the house. We carefully dropped each swatted fly into our cans.

When there seemed to be no more flies, we would take our cans to Mama and each of us would tell her how many we had. We knew better than lie to Mama; Mama knew everything. Mama would take the can and look inside for a moment. We were convinced she was carefully counting our flies. Then she would hand the can back and simply say, "Okay."

Lasting Impressions

Hay was a friendly little town where everyone knew everyone else. In the 1930s it consisted of a post office, general store, a gas station, grain elevator, a blacksmith shop, and two churches. The community was also proud of its comparatively new brick school building that accommodated all twelve grades.

The little, white church on the edge of town was constructed by a traveling evangelist, who was also a carpenter. My grandfather (Papa) had donated the land and provided the funds for building the church. It was in that little church I have memories of God reaching into my young life and touching me with His gracious Hand of love.

Occasionally a missionary family would come to the little church and tell of their work in Indonesia. Real live missionaries were a rarity. The community school always granted permission for the missionaries to tell of their adventures to the student body. Grades one through twelve would assemble in the gymnasium for those special occasions.

I often heard Papa speak of the W. W. Pattersons, the missionaries to Indonesia. This missionary family made an impression on me, especially since they had a little girl about my age. Their name stuck in my memory. Those were the first seeds of missionaries and their work that were planted in my young heart.

A Nightmarish Dream

One night when I was about eight years old, after I had climbed into bed, I was pondering in my heart how I could honor God. I had a desire to reach out to God in a more honorable way than my usual childish way of praying.

I loved the way Grandma prayed. Her soft, sweet voice was like the person she was. I was always impressed with all the "thees" and "thous" that graced Grandma's prayers. When Papa prayed, the words tumbled out so fast they all seemed to merge into one. I never could understand anything Papa had prayed.

That night I determined to pray like Grandma prayed. With a desire to show honor to God, I struggled to include "thees" and "thous" in my prayer. They were unfamiliar words to my vocabulary, so using them in my prayer didn't come easy. Then I fell asleep.

I had a terrible nightmarish dream that night. I dreamed evil beings like men were chasing me. I ran and ran through dark, drab, unpainted barns and buildings. All the buildings seemed to be in close proximity. This was unfamiliar territory I had never seen before. Wherever I ran, those evil men were still after me.

I awoke in a sweat, extremely frightened. In my heart I knew this frightening dream was from the devil. He was trying to discourage me from ever again wishing to show honor to God. I fell asleep again only to have the nightmare continue in the same manner. I was alone—running and running from evil men, running in and out of those dark, unpainted barns and buildings. Again I awoke in a sweat, horribly frightened.

My sister Zella and I slept together in a double bed. We never had enough resources for each of us to have our own bed. The double bed made it convenient when overnight guests would come. At those times my sister and I would give up our bed and sleep on the floor.

That night Zella continued to sleep soundly on her side of the bed. I was so frightened I took hold of a corner of her pajamas for some kind of security. I was careful not to awaken Zella. Somehow I dropped off to sleep again, but found myself still being chased and still running.

Then the dream suddenly changed. It became a peaceful, quiet scene. A very graceful lady came out of a peaceful home and knelt in the beautiful lawn. I considered her to be Chinese because of her oriental clothing. Then the dream ended.

For many nights after that dream, I was still very frightened. It was summertime and very hot in the attic-like room where we slept. Even then I would pull the sheet up over my head and secretly take hold of a corner of Zella's pajamas after she had gone to sleep. I hung on tightly so those evil beings couldn't come and pull me away. I was too timid to tell Daddy and Mama about the frightening dream.

Paradise around Us

We never envied those who lived in the confines of a city. The wonderful hills around us held much pleasure. In the spring we would roam the hills looking for spring flowers—buttercups, birdie-bills, and bluebells. As spring gave way to summer, the three of us children would beg to go barefoot. Mama would feel the ground, and if it passed her good judgment of being warm enough, she would allow us to take our shoes and socks off.

We would go barefoot all summer long. By the end of summer, our feet were so toughened it was very uncomfortable to put on shoes and socks. But uncomfortable or not, shoes and socks were required when school started again in the fall.

And then there was winter time. During the winter snows, those wonderful hills became a paradise for sledding. Our own private sledding paradise was just up the hill from the house.

Broader Horizons

We lived in this wonderful paradise until I was eleven. In the summer of 1943, for various reasons, there was an exodus from Hay of a number of families. They were all reaching out for broader horizons. Our family was among the exodus. At the end of the summer, we moved to a small town in the Yakima Valley in the central part of Washington State where Daddy bought a thirty-acre ranch.

Instead of rolling wheat hills, now we were surrounded by fruit orchards, grape vineyards, asparagus fields, hop fields, and all the other many things the irrigated valley produced.

When school was out for the summer months, we three kids worked at many jobs. The meager wage of swatting flies in our younger years was exchanged for seventy-five cents an hour for cutting asparagus or working in the hop fields. Picking cherries for three cents a pound became our most lucrative job.

Daddy and Mama taught us to work diligently. They also taught us how to properly value the money we earned from our hard work. Giving to God the first ten percent of what we had earned was a principle Daddy and Mama instilled deeply into us.

After High School

After graduating from high school in 1949, I enrolled in Prairie Bible Institute in Canada. I attended there for two years. Missionaries were often invited to speak to the student body to tell of their experiences on the mission field. Hearing different missionaries tell their stories deepened my desire to follow God wherever He might lead me.

During my second year in Bible school, a very exciting event happened in our family. I received a much anticipated telegram from Daddy, "Samuel Nathan arrived at one this morning." A new baby brother had joined us. Eighteen years earlier I had been the last such event in our family.

The Fall of 1951

Following the two years in Bible school, I went to Los Angeles, California, in the fall of 1951, to attend a short-term soul winning training school. This training school was for people of all ages and all walks of life who desired to be more effective in personally telling others of the blessings of Christ's salvation.

It was during this three-month training course that I had very sincerely responded to a challenge for missionaries to go to Japan. God had moved very deeply in my heart and I responded in sincerity and commitment to His will, "Lord, I'm going to Japan unless You close the door."

My cousin Wilma and I attended the soul winning training school together. She, too, had been among those who responded to the challenge of going to Japan as a missionary.

Wilma and I were more than just cousins. Our fathers were brothers and our mothers, sisters. Our families had always been very close. Wilma's family, too, had lived at Hay during her young childhood. The same year we moved from Hay to the Yakima Valley, their family had moved to Spokane, Washington.

Journey Home

When the three-month training course was completed in December, Wilma and I returned to our homes in Washington State. Each of us would tell our parents we wanted to go to Japan to be a missionary.

We took the Greyhound Bus for the long, thirty-hour journey home. At Portland, Oregon, we changed buses. A snowstorm was overtaking us, so snowy weather was expected for the rest of the journey. The bus we were now on was going to Spokane through Ellensburg. Spokane was Wilma's destination. I had to again change buses at Toppenish, Washington, which was just thirty miles from my home. That bus would go down through the Yakima Valley. My destination was Prosser. A few other passengers at the Toppenish depot were waiting for the same bus.

Journey Becomes a Nightmare

Up to this point, my bus journey was uneventful. The rest of the journey, just thirty more miles, turned out to be a nightmare.

The bus I was waiting for was caught in the snowstorm. No one knew when it would arrive. It was now about 9 p.m. The lobby of an old hotel was the bus depot's waiting room. It was a dark, dingy, dismal place—the kind of hotel lobby that had a spittoon in one corner. In that dismal place, I began feeling so alone.

After waiting for some time, I finally tried calling home. My family didn't readily make phone calls in those days from the distance I was attempting to call. In spite of the snowstorm, could they possibly come and get me? But no one heard the phone. Everyone at home was already bedded down for a long, winter's nap. I was so close to home and yet so far away.

As the hours ticked away in that dismal place, I began feeling a different kind of darkness closing in on me. It was a similar darkness to the very frightening, nightmarish dream I had as a young girl. Here I was again, desiring to fully honor God with my life. I felt those same evil forces in the nightmarish dream pressing in upon me and taunting me. Only this time it wasn't a dream—it was real life.

The few other passengers waiting for the snow-delayed bus began talking of getting a taxi to take them to Grandview. They wondered if I would like to join them. Grandview would put me within five miles of home. It was a ray of hope.

Someone called the taxi and about five of us piled in with our bags and baggage. We all shared in paying the taxi fare.

In Grandview the others scattered to their various places. The only place I had to go was the bus depot. This time it was in a small all-night cafe. It was not the kind of place a young lady would choose to be alone, especially in the wee hours of the morning. But there I was. Again I tried calling home. Now I was only five miles away. Surely someone would hear the phone! But the long, winter's nap still had everyone sound asleep.

Those evil, harassing forces continued to taunt me. A terrible darkness and loneliness engulfed me. I felt so out of place. As the hours ticked away, only the waiter and waitress were now in the cafe.

At some point during those dreadful waiting hours, a gang of young guys came stomping in. A short, stocky guy who seemed to be the gang leader filled the place with his arrogant attitude. Before stomping back outside, he came over to where I was sitting and vented some of his arrogant, cocky feelings on me. In essence it was, "Who are you and what are you doing here?" My emotions were further shattered.

At 3:00 a.m. the delayed bus finally arrived at Grandview. A short ride to Prosser and again I and my suitcase were set out in the snow. At this hour the bus depot in Prosser was closed. But someone was aroused.

I was told that an old man with an old truck would sometimes transport stranded passengers to nearby locations. The old man was summoned with his rickety, old truck. He kindly transported me the last mile of my journey home. It was now 4:00 a.m. My calling from outside Daddy and Mama's bedroom window did what the phone had failed to do. They were jolted from their long, winter's nap. I was now in Daddy and Mama's loving care. At last I was *home.*

I Shared My Plans with Daddy and Mama

I was undaunted by the nightmarish journey I had just gone through. I had made a covenant with God that I would go to Japan as a missionary, and He had flooded me with peace. I continued to trust Him to guide me.

I shared with Daddy and Mama my desire to honor God with my whole life. I told them of the urgent challenges that had been given for missionaries to go to Japan. I told them how I had responded, how I had sincerely prayed from my heart, "God, I'm going to Japan unless you close the door." I told them of the peace that filled my heart then, and how that peace still reigned in my heart. Just as I knew they would, Daddy and Mama accepted my decision to go to Japan as a missionary. Their response was kind and helpful.

It was December. The mission board at the training school in Los Angeles had scheduled Wilma and me on a freighter, which would leave from the Port of Seattle for Japan in mid-May. Freighters usually had a few staterooms for passengers. They were less expensive than such accommodations on the big passenger liners.

There was much to do to get ready for the scheduled departure in mid-May. Wilma and I were each responsible for our own ship fare and for raising promised monthly support for our missionary venture. We also had to secure a passport and a visa, get required inoculations, and purchase household goods that we were advised to take along. The list was long. We would be in Japan for a five-year period without returning for a furlough.

Some people stood on the sidelines watching and wondering. I was sometimes asked, "What are you going to do about getting married?" I don't remember what I answered them, but I well remember what I said in my own heart, "I'm twenty now (my birthday was in March). In five years I will be twenty-five. That's not too old to get married." I never let the thought bother me in the least.

A number of our friends who had been in the training school in California were also making quick preparations for their departures to Japan within months. Some were in teams of four or five. Wilma and I were alone for our scheduled departure.

By now the mission we were with had a group of over forty missionaries in Japan. This was exciting. Wilma and I would soon join them. All of them were located on the island of Kyushu, Japan's southernmost of its four main islands. Kyushu was considered one of the least evangelized areas of Japan.

Daddy's Battle

From the time I told Daddy and Mama I was going to Japan as a missionary, they did everything they could to help me. In the following years, I heard many missionaries tell how family members had stood against them in obeying their missionary call. With gratefulness I always made mention how my parents had done everything they could to encourage me. It wasn't until I had been in Japan for twenty-five years, that one day Daddy told me of the great battle he had in letting me go to Japan.

Here is Daddy's story: *"Was Phyllis' going to Japan really God's will? Since she was so young and a single girl, would it be right for me, as her father, to allow her to go? At first I comforted myself that it would be impossible for Phyllis to raise the needed support for going to Japan. Therefore, circumstances would take care of the situation, and it wouldn't be necessary to confront her."*

Not knowing anything of Daddy's battle, I plodded on with every intention of leaving for Japan in May. Little by little my needs were being supplied. People began talking to Daddy, "You should never allow her to go. She's too young. She's not married. Who will support her? It's your duty as her father to stop her!"

Daddy and Mama were both very dedicated to God and His will. They desired only God's will for us children. Daddy said the battle in his heart of whether my going to Japan was really God's will or not raged day and night. Often it was with tears flooding his eyes. If only he knew for sure it was God's will.

As Daddy related it to me, several times he decided he must talk to me. He must tell me he didn't think I should go to Japan, at least not until I was a little older and better prepared. He said he knew I would obey his advice.

Daddy said each time he made the decision to talk with me to discourage me from going to Japan, he would see his own hand reaching out to take the little girl off the altar where he had placed her many years ago. This stopped him short of saying anything to me. Daddy had no intentions of going back on his promise to God to *"give her to You for all the days of her life."*

The battle still raged in his heart. *"If only I knew her going to Japan was really God's will. It's dangerous in Japan. The war has been over such a short time. The Korean Conflict is on and could boil over into Japan. She isn't married. I am her father. It's my responsibility to stop her."*

Daddy said he shared his battle with no one—not even Mama. Then one night Daddy had a dream. He dreamed he was helping carry my suitcases to the ship. He picked up one of the suitcases and it appeared to be empty. He called my attention to it. He said I simply replied, "No, Daddy, I don't have anything to put in that one." In his dream Daddy noticed something written in small letters on the suitcase. Looking closely he saw the word "Sorrows."

Daddy immediately awoke from his dream. He was assured that God's gracious Hand would be upon me. With tears and thanksgiving of heart, he cried out, *"O God, you have shown me it is Your will. You can have her. She can go to Japan, even if I never see her face again."*

Daddy's battle was over. A few months later, with peace of heart, Daddy was able to say farewell as I left for Japan.

Voyage to Japan

On May 15, 1952, Wilma and I boarded the ship at the Port of Seattle. This was the ship that would take us on our anticipated journey to Japan. Daddy, Mama, and my little brother Sammy, who was now a year and half old, were there at the ship to bid us farewell. Wilma's parents were there. My brother Paul, who was attending Bible school in Seattle, was there. Wilma's and my grandparents,

Time with Daddy and Mama just before
I boarded the ship at Seattle

Dad and Ma Poe, were all there. It was not a sad farewell. Wilma and I were excited to be going. The well-wishers, for the most part, withheld their tears as they observed our enthusiasm.

A few days earlier at a family gathering, Dad had prayed a prayer that continued to bless me. I gratefully held it in my memory. Dad prayed, *"O God, I am so honored to have two granddaughters who are going to the mission field."* My dear grandpa, whom I respected so highly, was proud that Wilma and I were embarking on missionary careers. I continually treasured my wonderful Christian heritage of my parents and grandparents.

After the farewells were all said and the gangplank was pulled up, the ship slowly moved away from the dock. By now it was evening. Wilma and I were leaving all that was familiar and headed toward a land we knew very little about. I knew God had called me, and I knew He would faithfully lead me into His entire plan.

Our ship, the *Ocean Mail*, was a very nice, freight vessel of the American Mail Lines. There were twelve staterooms for passengers. Wilma and I shared a room. These rooms were first class accommodations, including dining with the officers of the ship.

The next morning when we awoke, the great Pacific Ocean was our only scenery. Indeed we were out at sea. How exciting to be on our way to Japan. Even though I grew up in Washington State, I had never seen the ocean. For some reason the word "whitecaps" had always intrigued me. That first morning of our voyage, Wilma and I went out on deck. I wanted to see whitecaps. But not a whitecap was in sight; the ocean was calm.

The next morning, still not a whitecap. And the next morning and the next. The ocean continued to be calm all the way to Japan. Not seeing a single whitecap was somewhat of a disappointment to me. The voyage from Seattle to Japan usually took fourteen days, but because of the smooth ocean, our ship made it in twelve.

On the morning of the twelfth day, a speck of land was sighted. We were told it was Japan. One of the passengers had a pair of binoculars. She very kindly let all of us take turns looking as that speck became a larger mass of land. I will never forget the feeling that welled up within me when, a short time later through the binoculars, I could discern terraced rice fields on the mountain sides. That was something I had only seen in geography books. Now I was seeing terraced rice fields for real.

By mid-afternoon our ship slid into Yokohama Harbor. We anchored out in the harbor among many other ships from many other places. All through the voyage, it had seemed as though no one shared the ocean with us. Now we were sitting in the middle of a world of ships.

We had arrived in Japan on May 27, 1952. Wilma and I with all our baggage and crates weren't scheduled to disembark until the next stop, which would be Kobe. Kobe was south of Yokohama and considerably closer to Kyushu Island, which was our destination.

When we arrived at Yokahama, it was the beginning of Japan's rainy season. It rained and it rained and it rained. For the unloading of some cargo, rain would not have been a problem. But we learned our cargo was sugar! Those were the days before containers. Our ship sat in Yokohama Harbor for a week before the precious cargo could be safely unloaded.

Wilma and I shortly after we arrived in Beppu, a tourist town filled with hot springs. Steam is rising behind us.

Arriving at Our Destination—Beppu City

At last our ship was on its way to Kobe where Wilma and I disembarked. Some of our fellow missionaries who were living in the Kobe area welcomed us into their home for a few nights. They assisted us in getting our crates and baggage sent by train to the city of Beppu, Kyushu Island. Beppu was the location of the headquarters of our mission in Japan. Wilma and I were also assisted in getting on the train that would take us on the long ride to Beppu.

At Beppu fellow missionaries were busily bustling about with the wonderful opportunities of evangelism all around us. It was intriguing. This is what we had come to Japan to do. Although each of them had only recently arrived in Japan, to Wilma and me they seemed to be seasoned missionaries. They shared with us newcomers some of the "hows" and "how nots" and the "whys" and "why nots" concerning living in Japan.

Most of the mission's forty missionaries were scattered around Kyushu Island. Shortly after Wilma and I arrived, we learned all the missionaries would be gathering together within ten days at Sasebo for a missionary conference.

The mission director asked Wilma and me to help at the Beppu mission office until after the conference. Later he would assist us in getting located in a mountain village so we could start our missionary evangelism for which we had come to Japan. Wilma and I had thought we would probably be working at a location with a few other missionaries. Hearing we would be in a mountain village to start our own missionary work made us shudder a bit. But we took hold of courage and determined we could do what was required of us.

While we were helping out for those few days in the mission office, a cablegram was delivered. It was for a fellow missionary, Leo Kaylor, who was located in the southern part of Kyushu. The cablegram was informing Leo that his mother had passed away. Sadness came into the office knowing one of our members was receiving this very sad news.

Adjusting to a New Culture

On our arrival in Japan, we were abruptly introduced to a very unfamiliar culture, just as we had expected. We learned to take our shoes off at entry ways. We learned how to sit with our legs doubled under us on *tatami* (straw mat) floors. We learned to drink green tea and more green tea from tiny cups without handles. These were all easy adjustments. The accomplishment of these somehow made us feel like real missionaries.

The greatest adjustment, though, was the toilet facilities. These facilities were usually inside the house. They called it the *"benjo."* The *benjo* consisted of a tiny closet with a hole in the floor. Inside the little closet, you squatted over the hole and did your business. A large crock-like container under the floor held the contents.

Every month or so when the container became full, it was emptied through an opening from outside. The contents was dipped out into wooden buckets and carried away. It was sometimes used to "freshen" the gardens! In modern Japan that procedure of freshening the gardens has been eliminated.

The smell that was created when the contents of the containers was removed and carried away was very obnoxious and penetrating. Foreigners ironically dubbed those wooden buckets *"honey buckets."* That was over fifty years ago. A few of those *benjo* still remain. But most of Japan has now been converted to the flush toilet system.

Another challenge for newcomers to Japan was learning to use Japanese money. The yen that had been issued for our dollars consisted mostly of paper money. A handful of money wasn't worth much. In those days the only coins represented the smallest denominations of yen—one coin was worth about one fourth of a penny and another about half that value.

When we wanted to make a purchase at one of the many, small, open shops or markets that dotted the streets, we would try out some of the first words we learned, *"Ikura desu ka?"*— ("How much is it?"). Not yet able to understand the answer to that question, we were compelled to hold out some paper money in our hand. The shopkeeper would take the necessary amount. They appeared trustworthy so we trusted them. Through the years we learned the Japanese, because of their respect for the virtue of trust, would find it difficult to be dishonest in those circumstances.

The Missionary Conference

Our mission had scattered their missionaries in towns and villages along the seacoasts that circled Kyushu Island. Most of the central part of Kyushu is very mountainous. Sasebo, where our conference would be held, is located on the northwest side of Kyushu near Nagasaki. It was a happy, exciting day when all the missionaries gathered at Sasebo for a few days together. Wilma and I were welcomed as the newest newcomers.

The accommodations for our conference were very simple, as was most everything that touched our lives in those days. The building that had been secured for the conference was a big, shed-type building that the U.S. naval forces had temporarily used. The women slept in one large room and the men in another. Each of us had a simple mat, a simple pillow, and a simple covering. The little that it was sufficed since we were in the warm weather of June.

One morning I was on my way to wash my face at the mutual washing place. I went to get my hand towel from an unfinished wall where I had hung it. There was a big, black, worm-looking thing clinging to my towel. Just the sight of it seemed to demand some respect. I shook it off my towel and it disappeared through one of the cracks in the floor.

Later, since the sight of that worm-looking thing was imbedded in my mind, I described it to one of the ladies. She exclaimed, "Oh, that was a centipede! Centipedes have a poisonous, very painful sting." Indeed, that black, worm-looking thing did demand some respect!

During our few days together, all of the missionaries thoroughly enjoyed sharing their many and varied experiences. Wilma and I listened and learned. Relaxing in our English language was a luxury for those who had now been in Japan for several months or more.

Leo Kaylor, who had received the cablegram about his mother's death, was also at the conference. He was a handsome, young man from Arkansas who seemed to stand out in the crowd. I was impressed with his sincere dedication to God and his kindly, cheerful mannerisms.

Located in a Mountain Village

After returning from the conference, just as the mission director had informed us, Wilma and I were thrown into the big responsibility of getting located in a mountain village not far from Beppu.

Takeda was a quaint, little village nestled in the Aso Mountains. A tunnel connected one part of the village to the other. We rented some rooms in a school teacher's home on the side of town that required traversing through the tunnel.

The mission director had arranged for a young, Christian, Japanese girl to go along as our interpreter. The vice-mayor of the village befriended us. He reached out a protective, fatherly hand toward us, probably because of our youth. We deeply appreciated his kindnesses.

High school students swarmed around us eager to learn English. After getting settled in our rented rooms, we announced Bible classes would be started in our living room. There was always a group of high school students who attended.

Some months later the mission director came out to Takeda to check on us. He was impressed with the response our Bible classes were having. Before he returned to Beppu, he told us, "These students are sincere in their faith. You should teach them about baptism. I will come back and baptize them." Later we did have a baptismal service for several students. We were encouraged with the beginnings of our missionary careers.

About this time the mission director sent another young lady, who had just arrived in Japan, to join Wilma and me at Takeda.

Summertime Heat and Humidity

By the end of July, all of us newcomers to Japan were learning how exhausting Japan's summertime heat and humidity can be. Also, the reality of how desperately we needed to learn the language was descending upon all of us.

In view of this, the mission director decided we would all do well to get away from the intense heat for a few weeks and spend some time concentrating on learning the language. An ideal location was found in the Kirishima Mountains in southern Kyushu.

This camp site consisted of newly-constructed bungalows and kitchen facilities for a large group. There also was a two-story building we would use for Japanese lessons in the large upstairs room, and for a dining area on the first floor. The facilities would be available for our missionary group after the first of August.

It would be a week before August arrived. To help those of us who had most recently come to Japan, two young men in Miyazaki offered their spacious rented house for a week of language study. This was a welcome plan as all of us were desirous to delve into the language. About ten of us missionaries converged upon the young men's house. One of those who had invited us was Leo Kaylor.

We studied Japanese in the mornings and used afternoons to try to digest what we had been taught. In the evenings we sometimes went out for street meetings. Other evenings we would have worship and prayer together.

One leisurely evening, with the sun still a distance from the horizon, Leo approached me and asked if I would like to go for a walk! Without hesitation I answered, "Yes." Leo's personal expression toward me came as a bit of surprise. I wasn't aware he had any interest in me.

Leo led me along a little pathway that took us up to an elevated river embankment not far from the house. It was a wonderful, grassy place to sit. A pleasant, cool breeze added perfection to the occasion. I have no remembrance of what we talked about. But I could be rather sure it centered on Leo's burden for ministering in Japan. That was his heartbeat. My admiration for Leo deepened.

Kirishima

As was planned, the first of August all of us forty or fifty missionaries gathered at the Kirishima camp site. We left the stifling heat down below. The pleasant air of the Kirishima Mountains was refreshing. With comfortable temperatures, a few camping inconveniences didn't matter much.

We would be spending a month in this cool mountain area for the purpose of studying the language. The bungalows we lived in were of the simplest construction with nothing but a door, a window, bare-board walls, and *tatami* (straw mat) floor.

When it rained all the walkways among the bungalows turned to mud. *Geta* became our most popular footwear. *Geta* are wooden clogs that elevate you slightly off the ground. Japanese primarily used *geta* for their footwear in those days. Shoes were saved mainly for special occasions.

Our gathering was a mixed multitude. Families with children, grandpas and grandmas, the middle aged, and many young people defined our group. We were all from varied walks of life, but we shared the same purpose for coming to Japan—ministering the gospel to the Japanese. We also shared the same desire to learn the language so we could be more effective in our ministry.

A Budding Romance

Kirishima became a wonderful place for two young people who found themselves more and more attracted to each other. On leisurely, good-weather afternoons, Leo often asked if I would like to go for another walk. Getting acquainted with this godly young man I respected so highly was beyond my expectations. In fact, I didn't have any expectations. I had set them aside when I committed myself to come to Japan for five years.

The month in the mountains was coming to an end. Our efforts at studying this very difficult language paid off to some degree. Everyone was getting anxious to go back down the mountain to their locations of ministry.

Leo was planning to move from Miyazaki to start evangelizing in a new city. He would be going alone to the southwestern side of Kyushu to the small city of Sendai. I was located on the northeastern side of the island.

The evening before he left, Leo asked me again to go for a short walk up a mountain trail with him. We sat on some rocks along the trail. By now each of us had a heart full of feelings for the other. "I would like to write to you. Could I suggest we write each other once a week?" Leo shared his desire with me. We didn't know how long it would be before we would be together again. Writing was a welcome plan, a plan that would help make parting a bit easier.

I Shared My Joys with Daddy and Mama

In my weekly letters to Daddy and Mama, I spilled out the news that a very special friend had come into my life. Daddy remarked in a return letter that he and Mama had always prayed for each of us children that God would choose mates for us. They committed Leo's and my friendship into God's guidance.

Now, here I was walking on one of life's very important pathways that had been made smooth by Daddy and Mama's prayers. Though a great expanse of ocean separated us, Daddy and Mama continued to be my source of counsel and security.

Back Down the Mountain

All of us missionaries left the cool refuge in the Kirishima Mountains where we had been for the month of August. Down from the mountains, into the stifling heat of the summer, everyone scattered to their own place of ministry. Wilma and I headed to northern Kyushu. It was a long, hot train ride back to the little, mountain village of Takeda.

Trains in those days were pulled by coal-fueled steam engines. There, of course, was no air conditioning. In the hot summer, all windows on the train would be opened. The hot wind through the windows was better than no wind. But tunnels posed a problem and mountainous Japan has many. When the train entered a tunnel, suddenly all windows were closed in an attempt to keep the coal smoke out. Nevertheless, the black smoke seeped into the coach in spite of closed windows. It hovered around us until the train exited the tunnel. Then all the windows were thrown open again. The perspiration on faces and arms mixed with the black coal smoke served to create a darkened complexion on all the passengers!

Living alone in Beppu. God was faithfully with me.

New Assignment

Since another young lady had joined Wilma and me at Takeda, there were now three of us. Because of this the mission director asked if I would come back to Beppu and help in the mission's office. I much preferred to be out in direct ministry, but I obediently did as I was asked.

With the help of other missionaries in the Beppu area, I found a room I could rent in the home of a Japanese family. It was near the building where the mission had their office. In the same building, the mission had started a Bible school to train young people for the ministry.

During the day I was surrounded by others and I enjoyed the fellowship. But at night I was all alone, miserably alone. The family in whose home I had rented the room was very kind to me. But my use of the language was limited. In my timidity I kept to myself.

God allows us to be in lonely situations at times. It is a testing ground. Loneliness can be vulnerable. It's at such times we must learn to cling to God and trust in His faithfulness. As I reflect on that lonely period of time, I now realize God was at work. He was, indeed, going ahead of me working out His very special plan. His gracious Hand was upon me.

Along with the office work, one of my responsibilities was to get the mission mail every day from our designated box at the post office. The post office was a distance away, but I enjoyed the walk. One day among all the other pieces of mail, there was a letter addressed to me. It was from Leo! My heart leaped out of my aloneness. I could feel a joyful smile spread all over my face. I was aware I was very likely being watched since I was the only foreigner in the post office. But my smile kept smiling. I couldn't wait to open the letter. A bench was nearby, so I sat and continued smiling through Leo's entire letter—a nice, long one.

There were no romantic expressions in the letter. But that didn't matter. Leo was sharing his heart with me about his ministry. That was romantic to my heart!! And besides, at the end he wrote, *"Please send me a letter soon."* That also registered romantic to my heart.

Autumn

Hot summer had faded away. Now Japan's wonderful fall weather was our daily pleasure. Fruits and vegetables had often been in slim supply in the summertime markets. But with fall came an abundance of produce.

Mandrin oranges with their rich orange color brightened the roadside markets. Shiny, dark brown chestnuts, big and fat, added their beauty to the overflowing display of produce.

Up until now persimmons had been an unknown fruit to most of us foreigners. Japan had developed a large, sweet persimmon by the process of grafting. This delicious, fall fruit became a favorite. We learned early on to ask if the particular persimmon we had chosen at the market was of the sweet variety.

Many times the sweet persimmons and the puckery persimmons were displayed side by side. To our unaccustomed eye, we couldn't tell the difference. One experience of taking a bite of a puckery persimmon is sufficient for life!

But the puckery persimmons did have a special use. They were peeled, strung on strings, and hung under the eaves of the house to dry. Time and chilly weather turned the puckery persimmons into a delicious, sweet, dried fruit.

Rice harvest was one of Japan's most heartwarming seasons. The rice crop, with its many stages, had been well labored over since late spring when the seedbeds were prepared. The young rice plants were transplanted by hand in the flooded paddies about

June. Relatives and friends turned out to help the farmer with this time consuming job. Then the watchful eye of the farmer protected his crop until harvest time.

For much of Japan, rice harvest occurs in October. Again relatives and friends turned out to help the farmer. The cut stalks were tied together in bundles and hung over bamboo poles for a few days. We were told that was to let the rice cure. Many farmers did it that way in those days. The harvested rice paddies brought heartwarming serenity to the countryside.

Much has changed in the rice production in the past fifty years. Now the farmer with a small, modern tractor and other equipment does most of the work himself. As in so many areas of Japanese life, they are always making improvements. They strive for perfection. The flourishing rice fields become a beautiful carpet of green, speaking forth that perfection.

Kindnesses of the Japanese

During that first fall in Beppu, every weekend I returned to Takeda to be a part of the ministry there. The trip required a change of trains at Oita. The first time I made this trip alone, I was quite apprehensive about making the right connections for the train to Takeda.

The Beppu ticket agent tried to be helpful with his detailed explanations. I understood only a little of what he said, but probably responded *"Hai"* (Yes). It can be an indirect way of saying "I understand" when you probably really don't. No doubt, my dubious facial expressions alerted him that I was uncertain. It has always been my lot that what I am feeling inside comes out clearly on my face, even if I try to impress otherwise.

When I got off the train at Oita to make the change, a station agent was there to meet me. The Beppu agent had alerted the Oita agents about my need to change trains and my need for help in doing so. I was very kindly escorted to the right train.

It was late afternoon and happened to be the time of day when school students were commuting back to their homes. Every coach was packed to the limit; there was no room for me and my suitcase. Seeing the situation, the kind station agent took me to the baggage car. He encouraged me to climb in. Several students had already availed themselves of the baggage car, but there was still room for me.

The students welcomed me. They invited me to sit on some of the baggage with my suitcase beside me. Though a bit perplexed at the time, I shall always remember with a smile the kindnesses that were shown me that day. We have lived with similar kindnesses all our years in Japan.

Letters and Visits

Leo's wonderful letters continued to come every week. Answering them was a pleasure. A month went by. The mission director called some of the men of the mission to come to the headquarters at Beppu for a business meeting. Leo was among those men.

Being together again was a wonderful unexpected blessing for Leo and me. When time permitted we went for more walks. Now there were no riverside paths or mountain trails. It was the busy, narrow streets of Beppu, a hot springs town known for its tourism.

We paid little attention to the many souvenir shops that lined the streets—our focus was on each other. We usually found a little shop along the way where we could order something simple to eat. There we would just sit and talk.

For the next several months, whether for a mission's meeting or just an excuse, Leo found his way up to Beppu about once a month. We chuckle as we look back now. Our courtship consisted of our weekly letters that went back and forth and Leo's monthly visits.

New Year's Conference

In the southwestern side of Kyushu where Leo was working, several of the missionaries planned a joint New Year's conference for the first of January. It would be held in Kagoshima. The missionaries and their believers would gather at the large, sprawling house that two missionary ladies had rented for their work. With ample facilities it would be ideal for the conference.

Leo had been assigned to be one of the leaders of the conference. In one of his letters to me, he asked if I could come and join him at the conference. Since it was in a different location than where I was working, I thought I should perhaps get the mission director's permission to go. He readily gave his permission.

As the missionaries and their believers gathered, the facilities of the large, sprawling house were packed out. How encouraging to all the involved missionaries to see the response to the gospel that had been made. The meetings were filled with singing and praying and sharing and praying some more. How some of those young people prayed! They were intense in their faith.

A baptismal service was planned for some of the new believers. Permission had been granted to use a nearby public bathhouse for the service. This was ideal since it was January. Baptizing in the warm water was a welcome blessing. That is, except for one young man. The words for cold water and warm water are two different words in the Japanese language. When it refers to baptism in the Bible, it uses the word for cold water. This young man insisted he wanted to be baptized in cold water, just as the Bible states. A second baptismal service was arranged for him in the cold water of the ocean at the nearby beach.

The conference came to an end. It had been a wonderful time of fellowship and spiritual blessings. Missionaries with their believers scattered to the places from where they had come.

Perfect Setting for a Proposal

Leo had been very busy helping direct the conference. We had no time to spend together until after everyone left. At the invitation of the two missionary ladies in whose home we had gathered, Leo and I decided to stay with them another couple days.

That first evening together, we walked to the nearby beach. The tide was out. Several little fishing boats, each secured by a rope, were on the sandy shore. We chose one of the little boats for a place to sit.

Across the bay majestic Mt. Sakurajima loomed into the clear night sky. Though an active volcano, Mt. Sakurajima is a mountain of great beauty that rises out of the Kagoshima Bay.

Leo and I were thoroughly enjoying each other's company. God's majestic handiwork spread out in front of us. It was one of the most romantic settings two young people who were in love could ever wish for.

As we sat there, up from behind that breathtaking mountain rose the most gorgeous, full moon you could ever imagine. Moonbeams shimmered across the quiet bay pointing to the little boat right where we were sitting. We were in awe by the wonder and beauty of it all. God seemed to be smiling upon us.

I always deeply appreciated Leo's desire to focus upon God in our times together. Along with whatever romantic conversation we carried on, we quoted chapters of the Bible to each other that we had memorized in recent months. We lingered for some time in this very romantic setting. It was an absolutely perfect time and place for the proposal we were both ready for.

On such wonderful romantic occasions, time slips by unnoticed. We finally decided it was probably time to return to our friends' home. As we looked around us, to our utter dismay, we discovered the tide had come in. Although we were completely unaware of it, our little boat was now floating in the very still water!

We had no idea how deep the water was. There was nothing in the little boat with which we could measure the water's depth. Leo took off his shoes and socks and rolled up his pant legs. All he could do was see for himself how deep it was. He eased himself over the back of the little boat into the cold water, not knowing what to expect. Fortunately, the water was less than knee deep!

The wonder of that marvelous evening with God's blessings shining upon us has lingered on in our hearts. Mt. Sakurajima, to us, has become a symbol of those wonderful memories.

A Most Unlikely Place for a Proposal

Our special days together had come to an end. It was time for Leo and me to return to our separate places of ministry. We would be traveling together on the train for the first hour and a half. At Sendai Leo would get off the train. It would be another six hours further for me to arrive back at Takeda. I was planning to stop there for a few days before going on to Beppu to resume my duties at the mission office.

We boarded *The Kirishima* at the Kagoshima train station. This popular express train was starting out on its twenty-eight hour run to Tokyo. The New Year's holiday had ended and everyone else was also returning to their homes. Every inch of the train was packed with travelers. Standing space in the entryway of one of the coaches was all Leo and I could acquire for ourselves and our suitcases. That little entryway, too, was packed like sardines.

Fortunately, our standing space was in a corner. Leo could lean on the wall and steady both of us as the train rocked and reeled along. We passed through several tunnels. The coal smoke from the steam engines was added to the tobacco smoke in the jam-packed entryway. But romantic hearts are romantic, no matter the setting.

Our time together was fast slipping away. Leo would soon be getting off the train. We would be separated again for a time. In that very crowded, smoke-filled place, Leo suddenly asked the question he had been longing to ask, "I would like to ask if you would be my wife?" I don't remember my exact answer, but knowing my feelings, it was probably something like this, "I would consider it a great privilege to be your wife."

Leo had proposed! My heart danced in ecstasy. In such a place, there could be no kisses. Squeezing each other's hand a little more tightly was all the expression we could make of the love that was flowing between us. Leo and I still laugh together about a very romantic, absolutely perfect setting for a proposal as compared to a smoke-filled, crowded New Years train. I cherish Leo's proposal to me just the way it happened!

Wintertime

We had found the heat of our first summer in Japan very stifling because of the humidity. Now we were experiencing our first winter. Unlike northern Japan, winter temperatures in Kyushu don't often get below freezing. But because of the humidity, the icy fingers of the cold reaches deep into your bones.

People in Kyushu built their houses to be as cool as possible because of summer's heat. The cold of winter was just endured. As the cold pressed in, everyone simply added another layer of clothing. There was no way to heat the entire room—the *hibachi* and *kotatsu* served as the source of heat. The *hibachi* was a large crock into which hot, glowing pieces of charcoal were placed on a bed of ash. It served for warming your hands only.

In addition to the *hibachi* was the wonderful *kotatsu*. A *kotatsu* was a low table placed over a well in the floor. Like the *hibachi*, hot, glowing pieces of charcoal were arranged on a bed of ash in the well. A heavy blanket was placed over the table.

Sitting on the floor with your legs dangling in the well, you could pull the blanket over your lap. There was space in the well to keep your feet a distance from the glowing coals. This was a very enjoyable way of warding off those icy fingers that were forever reaching for you. Surprisingly, if your legs are warm, your whole body can seem warm. Drafty air moving rather freely through the rooms accommodated the use of charcoal. Gases from the burning charcoal can be dangerous unless there is good ventilation.

In modern Japan the *hibachi* has become only a memory of yesteryear. But the *kotatsu* lives on. It has been modernized. Nowadays, a little electric heat lamp is attached to the under side of the low, blanket-covered table. In winter the cozy *kotatsu* is still loved by many.

Japan rose quickly out of the ravages of war. Within a few years, conveniences the Japanese had never known before invaded almost every part of their lives. Houses are now built to keep out the heat and cold. Air conditioning for the summer and kerosene fan-heaters are the modern way of life for most homes.

Lillie

In January of 1953, another team of missionaries arrived. Among them was a young lady born to Japanese parents in California. She and her family had experienced the concentration camps for

Japanese in the U.S. during World War II. Lillie had dedicated herself to become a missionary to the land of her ancestry. She spoke rather fluent Japanese, while most of us were struggling with the beginnings of this difficult language.

Lillie would sometimes come by the mission office and sit for a time to chat with me. Her beautiful character and spirit shined through her sweet simplicity. Everyone loved Lillie.

About this same time, another attempt to aid the missionaries in learning the language was set up. A language school with qualified Japanese teachers was put into operation in Oita, which was about forty-five minutes around the bay from Beppu. How I wished I could avail myself of this wonderful opportunity to study the language.

My mind began churning. Lillie would be ideal as secretary in the mission office instead of me. Her use of the language would be a great asset. I was in the office by assignment and commitment, but not by my choosing.

I suggested my idea to the mission director. He was favorable. It hinged on Lillie's willingness to take on the duties in the mission office. Lillie was so gracious to do whatever she was asked. She seemed pleased for the unexpected assignment.

This sudden turn of events was a joyful day for me. Immediately I made plans to move over to Oita. A group of our missionaries had already moved into an old, rambling farmhouse in preparation for attending the language school. They welcomed me to join them. The old house was in a rural area of Oita. It was a short, local train ride to the location of our language school.

On weekends the missionaries who lived in the old farmhouse would go back to their mission stations for services and evangelism. During the week they would return to the old farmhouse and the language school. It was a very effective plan.

As it turned out, Lillie wasn't with us for long. She had only been in Japan about two years when she learned she had an advanced stage of cancer. A few months later Lillie passed away. It was a very sad day when all we missionaries gathered at Beppu to bid the final farewell to our dear friend Lillie.

Wedding Plans

Leo's wonderful letters continued coming. Sweet words were now mingled with his sharing about his ministry. Both brought much joy to my heart. We had decided we wouldn't disclose our engagement until we could be together again.

The first of February, Leo arranged to come to Oita where I was now located. We would have a few days together. Conveniently at that time, there was a gathering of the local missionaries. We shared the good news of our engagement. The response was joyful congratulations. What they were expecting had come to pass!

Leo and I spent the short time we had together making wedding plans. We decided the end of May would be an ideal time for the wedding. It would be before the rainy season arrived and the weather would likely be pleasant. Wednesday would probably be the best time of the week for missionaries to gather. We chose a Wednesday at the end of May. It turned out to be May 27. Later, reflecting on that date, I realized it was exactly a year from the day I had arrived in Japan at Yokohama.

I was the one who was asked what I would do about marriage if I went to Japan. I had simply said to myself, "I'll be twenty-five when I return to the U.S.—that's not too old to get married."

The gracious Hand of the Lord was upon me to bless me with His exceedingly great plan. It was far beyond what I could have dreamed. God had given me the very best in giving me Leo.

Marriage License

Among other things that needed to be done before our wedding on May 27 was to secure our marriage license. This required a trip in person to the American Consulate in Fukuoka in northern Kyushu. Leo and I made that trek on April 27, as it turned out.

At the consulate, after all the many papers were filled out, we were waiting for our marriage license to be issued. A big, burly, American man called us to a back room—a very drab, uninviting room it was. He laid his cigar down that he had been puffing on. He took a book in his hand and read some legal statements, none of which neither of us was fully comprehending. Then he asked us to stand and raise our right hands to swear that the said things were true. We were bewildered. The man's final statement was, "And now I pronounce you man and wife."

In our bewildered state, we told him we had only come to secure our marriage license. The justice of the peace, as he turned out to be, retrieved his cigar and replied, "We don't issue marriage licenses at the consulate. We just perform the civil marriage."

Leo and I finally recovered from the bewildered state. We couldn't keep from laughing as we left the consulate that day. It had been dutifully recorded in my passport that, as of April 27, 1953, my name was amended to read Phyllis Esther Kaylor. Leo and I, of course, didn't consider ourselves married. May 27 was the wonderful day we, in God's blessings, would be pronounced man and wife.

Making Decisions

We received permission from the Nazarene pastor in Beppu to use their little church building for our wedding. It was a very simple building. There were no rooms that could be used for dressing rooms for the bridal party.

One of our missionary ladies lived near the Nazarene church. She offered her apartment as a place for me and the bridesmaids to dress on the day of the wedding. That would mean I would be walking a few blocks to the church in my wedding dress on unpaved roads. Suppose it were a rainy day. I decided a long wedding dress would be impractical.

I had a seamstress in Takeda make my white, satin dress at calf length. I was now going back to Takeda more frequently. This gave opportunity to have the dress fit to perfection. The seamstress was very proud of her work. When she had finished my dress, she promptly displayed it in her shop window for the whole village to see.

My wedding dress on display in the middle of the village distressed me. I considered my marriage to Leo was very sacred. I went to the shop immediately, thanked the seamstress for her kindnesses, paid her for her excellent work, and took my wedding dress home.

Leo had asked one of the fellow missionaries to be best man and his Japanese interpreter that worked with him in Sendai to be a groomsman. I wanted Wilma to be my maid of honor, and I asked the wife of Leo's interpreter to also be in the bridal party. One of our older missionaries whom we greatly respected would walk me down the aisle in place of Daddy. Neither Leo's nor my family members could possibly come from the U.S. for our wedding.

The wedding ceremony would be given in English. A Bible school student would read the interpretation in Japanese. One of the missionary ladies would sing, *"Saviour, Like a Shepherd Lead Us"*. Another song would be sung in Japanese.

The Gracious Hand of the Lord Was upon Us

Leo and I firmly believed it was the gracious Hand of the Lord that had brought us together. We felt God's Hand of blessing upon us in our first days of friendship. The romantic walks in the Kirishima Mountains filled our hearts with more of those same blessings.

Leo's proposal in that crowded, smoky train in January was another time we felt the very precious and gracious Hand of the Lord upon us. Whether in a smoky train or on a sandy beach bathed in the light of a full moon seemed to make no difference to God—He was with us where we were. Now we were ready for our lives to be joined together. We knew that God would continue to bless and guide us in all that was ahead.

Our Wedding Day—May 27, 1953

Our wedding day arrived. It was blessed with pleasant weather. Missionaries came from all over Kyushu to rejoice with us. Before 2:00 p.m. Americans and Japanese began filing into the little Nazarene Church. It was a simple setting, but the ceremony was rich in spirit, depicting our hearts.

One of the missionary ladies wrote a detailed report of our wedding and sent it to the mission headquarters in Los Angeles. The report was printed in the mission's monthly publication. The pages of that publication are now yellow with age, but I will quote a few statements from it:

> Wedding time arrived. The church rapidly filled up with Americans and Japanese. The service that followed was the most truly satisfying Christian wedding ceremony most of us had ever witnessed--beautifully worded and Christ honoring. All of us felt the reverent spirit of love and consecration with which Leo and Phyllis entered their contract. Meanwhile, the wedding was giving a

real Christian testimony to the crowd of curious Japanese outside. They peered through the windows and strained for a glimpse of the strange service.

Our wedding day, May 27, 1953—Now Mr. and Mrs. Leo Kaylor

One of the missionaries had an idea. He had arranged for a rickshaw driver to come to the little church with his carriage. In those days a rickshaw was a two-passenger carriage propelled by a bicycle.

When the wedding was over and Leo and I radiantly exited, we were instructed to climb into the quaint rickshaw. In this extraordinary fashion, we were escorted to the Bible school building a few blocks away where the reception would be held. The rickshaw ride added laughter and pleasure to our wonderful wedding day.

SECTION III

Together in Life and Ministry

1953-1957
Early Days of Ministry

Our First Home Sweet Home

After our honeymoon Leo took me home. This was in south-western Kyushu in the town of Sendai of Kagoshima Prefecture. Home was a very humble, fifty-year-old farmhouse. It had recently been moved from far out in the country and situated on a small lot on the edge of Sendai.

The old farmhouse consisted of four rooms. If the sliding, paper doors separating them were removed, they would become one large square room. We made one room our living room, one a

Our first home sweet home

dining room, one our bedroom, and another a storage room. What more does a newly married couple need?

The four rooms were bordered by hallways. Sliding wooden shutters on the hallways consisted of our outside walls. Leo had to slide the wooden shutters open every morning. In the evening, in order to separate ourselves from the outside world, he had to slide them shut again. The importance of closing and locking all those wooden shutters at night was emphasized to Leo a short time before we were married.

One night Leo had decided to leave a few of the shutters partly open to allow night air to help cool the house. Very early the next morning, he was jolted awake by loud banging. Checking the situation Leo saw a policeman peering through the open space between the shutters. He thoroughly warned Leo of the dangers of not locking the house tightly shut at night. House robbery was a big problem in those days.

Leo had done his best to make this little old farmhouse as homey as possible before I arrived. I was happy he needed some help. How fulfilling for a new bride to put her feminine touch on the home and to experience how pleased her husband is with that touch.

Japanese Bath—*Ofuro*

Out on the edge of town where we lived, well water was the only water supply. We had to carry all our water from the community well across the street. It took many buckets to fill our bath. The bath (*ofuro*) consisted of a round iron tub encased in cement in the *ofuro* room. It was located just off the kitchen in a small, enclosed area that was space enough for bathing only.

For our baths the water was heated by a wood fire built under the iron tub. The fire-well was accessed from outside. Heating the bath was an intricate job. If the water got too hot, more water had to be carried from across the street. If the fire wasn't hot enough, a lukewarm bath had to suffice.

The process of a Japanese style bath is, first of all, dipping warm water out of the tub for soaping and rinsing off. There was a drain in the cement floor of the *ofuro* room. When you are clean, you get in the tub of water and relax in your hard-earned bath.

The tub was only big enough to sit in with your knees doubled up. But it was deep enough that the water would perhaps come to your shoulders. Everyone in the household uses the same tub of water. This suffices since all the soaping and rinsing off was done outside the tub.

As in days gone by, the process of the Japanese bath is the same to this day. But the ofuro room is now of streamlined beauty. Filling the tub and heating the water is controlled by a very sophisticated electrical system. Push a few buttons, wait a few minutes, and your wonderful *ofuro* is ready—filled and heated to perfection.

Well Water

When we first came to Japan, Japanese never drank what they called "raw" water. That was water that hadn't been boiled. They didn't even trust the water from the city water system to be drinkable. That is why they drank tea and more tea.

We knew this, but I didn't take it too seriously. We had been in Japan a year now, and drinking "raw" water never seemed to be a problem. But the well water we were now using was a very vulnerable source of trouble that we hadn't calculated.

One day a few months after we were married, I wasn't feeling too well. I stayed home and went to bed instead of joining Leo and the Christians at a hospital ministry. When Leo came home, he checked to see how I was feeling. When he bent down and gave me a kiss, he discovered I was burning hot with a fever. Every few minutes I would need to return to the *benjo*—the little cubicle with the hole in the floor. In a very short time, I didn't have the energy to get to the *benjo* without assistance. The situation was looking very grave.

Leo called the local doctor. When the doctor checked me, he diagnosed the problem to be dysentery. This was indeed a grave diagnosis, much feared by the Japanese. The doctor told Leo he had recently received some American medicine for treating dysentery. He said it was expensive but very effective. Leo asked the doctor to please use the medicine immediately. As soon as the medicine was administered, the aggressive dysentery was checked. I began mending from that moment.

The gracious Hand of the Lord, again, was certainly upon me. The doctor, with that very effective American medicine, was God's provision for our need.

That bout with dysentery took a toll on my physical body. In the few days I was affected, I lost about ten pounds, leaving me a mere ninety-eight pounds. It took a period of time before I regained my strength and weight.

Some years later when Leo and I were on our second furlough, we were visiting Leo's dad, John Kaylor, in Arkansas. One day while leisurely talking with him, I asked about his first wife. He told me the story. They had been in India a few years and were expecting their first child after six years of marriage. She was seven months pregnant when she contracted dysentery. They lived a day's journey from a hospital. No help was available. His wife died, and, of course, without medical assistance, the unborn baby died as well. That was 1917.

John Kaylor returned to the U.S. for a furlough after his seven and a half years in India were fulfilled. While he was in California, he met and married Ina Marshburn. John and Ina Kaylor then sailed for India in 1921 for another seven and a half years. Leo's brother and sister were born during that time. Leo joined the family in 1931, after his parents had again returned to the U.S.

Hearing this story I realized afresh that God's gracious Hand had been upon me, healing me of that bout with dreaded dysentery.

Ministry in Sendai

A nucleus of Christians was now forming in our church in Sendai. Our living room was the meeting place. Preparing the room for "church" was quite simple. Leo and I had very little furniture, just bare necessities. It was easy to move what little we had to one of the other rooms. Everyone then sat on the *tatami* (straw mat) floor in the 9' x 12' empty room.

In those days Leo used an interpreter for his Sunday messages. He studied the language daily in order to be on his own as soon as possible. Leo aggressively moved on in our church evangelism in spite of the handicaps of being dependent upon an interpreter. For personal witnessing though, he was now ministering on his own.

As the number of Christians increased, we needed more space for our church services. This was a gratifying problem. For more space, the sliding, paper doors between the living room and dining room were removed, making the room double the size it had been. We eventually bought folding, wooden chairs. This made a convenient situation for our church services.

When the services were over, the folding chairs were returned to our storage room, the sliding, paper doors were put back in place, and our furniture was arranged again in the living room and dining room. Our cozy little home was put together again.

A street meeting in Sendai. Mission Director preaching; Leo is praying.

Leo sharing the gospel with a farmer

Hospital Evangelism

Some of our evangelizing was done in hospitals where we were allowed to freely move from room to room telling patients about Christ.

In one room we found a young boy about eleven years old who was stricken with spinal meningitis. He loved for the big, tall missionary to come to his room and tell him about Jesus. In his simple way, Tetsuya San understood and accepted Jesus as his Savior.

In those days a family member stayed in the hospital with the patient to care for them. Because of this, Tetsuya San's grandmother was there. She listened politely as more of the story of Jesus was unfolded to them.

One day when Leo was talking with Tetsuya San and his grandmother, Tetsuya San went into one of his frequent convulsions. Leo laid hands on the stricken boy and prayed in the Name of Jesus for the convulsions to stop. Instantly they were gone. This convinced the grandmother that Jesus was the true and living God. She accepted Him as her Savior just as her grandson had done.

A blind friend of the grandmother came to the hospital to visit. The grandmother told her about the Jesus she now believed in. The blind friend spent hours listening to the grandmother retell the story of Christ's salvation. She had been searching for years for truth and peace of heart. A number of years previously, she had her eight year old son guide her on a pilgrimage. This was a well-known pilgrimage of visiting eighty-eight Buddhist shrines for the purpose of receiving enlightenment.

The shrines were located in isolated places on mountain tops and down in deep valleys. They were scattered throughout the islands of Kyushu and Shikoku. The blind lady and her son trekked for many months to pay a visit to each of these shrines. For her the end result of the pilgrimage was only confusion and disillusionment.

The blind lady began attending our church services to hear more of the story of Jesus. Her heart bore witness that this was the truth. She, too, became an ardent Christian and received the peace of heart for which she had been searching. Years later her son told us his dear blind mother died in her old age a very dedicated Christian overflowing with love and peace.

Sadly, over a period of about a year, we watched as Tetsuya San became weaker and weaker. One day one of the Christians rushed to our home and told us, "It seems Tetsuya San is gone." We hurried to the hospital and were there when the doctor confirmed that, indeed, he was gone. Tetsuya San had experienced, in his simplicity, a radiant faith in Jesus which had spilled over into the lives of others.

Chicken Pox

The following year after our marriage, I came down with an adult case of chicken pox. I wasn't exceedingly ill, but I was exceedingly covered with those itchy pox. I was literally covered from the top of my head to the bottom of my feet. In those miserable days, I sympathized with Job.

The medicine the doctor gave to help relieve the itch was a brown, muddy salve. I had to make a bed on the floor for myself to keep the "mud" from getting on the sheets of our bed. This isolation from Leo, though only a few feet away, was added misery. Of course my face wasn't spared. It was many days before I felt I was presentable enough to be seen in public again.

Blessings

The early months of 1955 were hinting that our wishes had come true. A trip to the doctor in March confirmed a baby was due in September. Leo and I were thrilled.

We were very encouraged with our church planting in Sendai. More people were being saved and more water baptisms in the nearby river. We were looking ahead for 1955 to be a wonderful year in the church. And now blessings were coming to our home, as well.

Occasionally, the terribly frightening dream I had as an eight year old child would come into my thoughts. When it did, I sometimes pondered what it must have meant.

One day not long after we were married, the dream was running through my memory. Suddenly I realized the graceful lady

Baptismal service at the river

in the peaceful scene at the end of that dream was dressed in a *kimono*. That meant she was Japanese and not Chinese, as I had mistakenly thought of her to be.

I sensed God in His gracious love was confirming to me that, indeed, Japan was His will for my life. It seemed He was telling me, "I put My call upon you when you were a child." I was overwhelmed with joy that God was confirming this to me, though I had never doubted I was in His will. Knowing assuredly you are in God's will gives you a firm anchor that holds you secure in Him whether you are in blessings or in troubles.

Trouble in the Camp

We had high expectations as we moved into our third year of ministry in Sendai. Then, in the spring of 1955, we began hearing disturbing rumors of the activities of Leo's interpreter. We learned he was secretly calling the members of the church to meetings we knew nothing about. He was beginning to sow seeds of discord among the believers.

Resentments against us by some of the church members began to surface. At the same time, loyalty to us and ill feelings against the interpreter were also being voiced. Soon the church was greatly shaken.

We decided we must release the interpreter of his responsibilities. By this turn of events, he rose up in great anger against us. Fortunately, he soon moved out of the area. In spite of all the shakings and rumblings, we were doing our best to hold fragments of the church together.

Leo determined he would never rely on an interpreter again. His determination helped him to press in that much more. He was continuing to improve in his ability in the language. He preached as he learned, and learned as he preached.

Just as things began to simmer down in the church, to our utter dismay, orders came from the mission headquarters in Los Angeles for us to move from Sendai. They knew nothing of the problems we were going through. They stated that, for the missionary, three years in one place was long enough. We were told that the Apostle Paul worked by this principle. We were instructed to leave the work with Japanese believers and move on.

Mission headquarters specified they wanted us to move to the large metropolis of Osaka-Kobe, and together with some other missionaries establish a work there. We were expected to do as they ordered. Such orders from mission headquarters without their fully understanding the missionary's situation were indeed shattering.

We were stunned. Loyalty to headquarters was our responsibility. At the same time, if ever the group of believers in Sendai needed us, it was now. With very heavy hearts, we set things in order as best we could. We left the church in the hands of the believers and moved to Osaka in June 1955.

We settled in an apartment in Osaka and tried to grasp the purpose of our being there. We were told to start a training center for young people to be trained for the ministry. Try as we might, nothing was working to produce that great goal. Nonetheless, Leo pressed on day by day to make contact with people to present the gospel to them. He worked diligently to follow up any contacts that looked promising of leading someone to Christ. We weren't necessarily discouraged with the limited results. We already knew ministering in Japan was with difficulty.

Our Tiny Bundle

Time was moving closer to our baby's due date which was calculated to be about September 9. A missionary doctor was to deliver our baby at an international hospital in Kobe. The hospital was about an hour away from where we lived. With three weeks until the due date, the doctor decided to go on vacation and would be back in plenty of time for our baby's arrival.

The evening of August 22, I began to feel an occasional bit of gnawing pain in my lower abdomen. But it wasn't time for the baby to come yet. That night the anxiety of new parents was our portion. We watched the clock. The regularity of the slight gnawing pains alarmed us. And then they subsided. And then they started up again. And then they subsided, only to start up again.

By now it was the early hours of the morning. Since we were an hour from the hospital, we decided perhaps we should go. That required arousing the kind missionary who lived nearby. Since he had a car, he said he would take us to the hospital when the time came.

On the drive to the hospital, he had a flat tire. We arrived at the hospital about 3:00 a.m. A substitute missionary doctor filled in for the doctor who was to have assisted at our baby's birth. Our tiny baby boy was born at 5:40 a.m. Robert Leo, a manly name for such a little fellow, weighed only 4 pounds, 8 ounces. It was August 23.

The substitute doctor was nervous, especially since the baby was so small. Delivering babies and caring for newborns was not his line of practice. He believed that mother's first milk was not best for the baby. However, the feeding he recommended proved very disruptive to the system of our little Robby.

For the next three days our baby cried. There was neither nursery nor incubator in the hospital—his little bed was in my room. The unusual diarrhea continued; the constant crying day and night was heart rending. Then our weak baby stopped crying altogether. That was worse.

Word of this tiny baby who was fighting for his life spread through the hospital. One after another, nurses would come in, peer down at our baby, and then leave shaking their heads. I watched every move they made hoping for some sign of hope. But they came silently and left silently.

The afternoon of the fourth day when Leo came for his daily visit, we went desperately before God. We walked down a hallway to a quiet place and poured out our hearts to God, "Our gracious God, please touch our little boy with your healing power."

By evening there was a noticeable change in Robby's condition. He began crying and sleeping normally, as a newborn baby should. The frightening diarrhea stopped. The gracious Hand of the Lord had come upon our baby and healed him. Thanksgiving and rejoicing poured from our hearts.

Robert Leo, born August 23, 1955. At six weeks he was still a tiny bundle, but healthy and growing.

First Furlough

Toward the end of 1955, the mission's department at the Los Angeles headquarters asked us to come home for their big missionary conference in December. This was unexpected as it wasn't time for our furlough yet. We were so excited to be going home. How proud I would be to introduce Leo and our precious, bright-eyed baby to my family. Robby was still small for his three and a half months, but he was healthy and active.

We planned to be in the U.S. for one year. We packed all our belongings and stored them in a warehouse made available to us. For various reasons we decided to fly home. The plane was a turboprop. In those days planes from Japan to Seattle stopped in the Aleutian Islands to refuel. When we were nearing Seattle, fog kept us circling overhead for about an hour before the pilot could get permission to land. That was a long hour.

Daddy, Mama, and Sammy, now five years old, had driven from Prosser to meet us when we came in. What a joyous reunion that was. Before I left for Japan, Daddy had agonized within himself if my going to Japan were really God's will. God stepped in through a dream and revealed to Daddy in a most unusual way that my going was truly His will. Daddy, in complete dedication to God had proclaimed, "O God, you can have her even if I never see her face again." When Daddy did see me again at the Seattle airport that night, he saw me standing beside my tall, handsome husband with a bright-eyed, little baby in my arms. Daddy wept tears of joy.

Days in the U.S.

Time changes things. Zella, Paul, and I were very close during our growing up days. Now we each had a family. Nevertheless, the closeness of our hearts remained the same. When Leo, Robby, and I arrived in the U.S. in 1955, Zella was bulging with the pregnancy of their third child. (She eventually had eleven.) Paul had married a year after Leo and I did; their little son was a few weeks younger than Robby. Daddy and Mama's house was abuzz with grandbabies when we all got together.

In late winter Leo, Robby, and I made a trip by car to visit Leo's family. His father lived in Arkansas, brother Roy and family in Texas, and sister Eilene and family in Tennessee. For me I had only known them as names and pictures. Now they were real people—Leo's family. God's blessings are upon families—it was a very special blessing for me to meet Leo's.

After spending time with the families in their various locations, we then headed north to Chicago to visit Leo's Uncle Perry and Aunt Addie. Uncle Perry's grand title was Dr. P. B. Fitzwater. He had been a professor of theology at Moody Bible Institute for over forty years but was now retired. What a privilege for me to meet that stately, elderly gentleman. Uncle Perry passed away about a year later.

Having accomplished all our travels across the U.S., we finally arrived back at Daddy and Mama's in Washington.

For the rest of our furlough, the mission headquarters had asked Leo to help out in the mission's department in Los Angeles. A small house in South Gate on the outskirts of Los Angeles was provided for us.

In December 1956 we made a trip back to Washington to spend Christmas with Daddy and Mama and the rest of the family. Our plans were to return to Japan in February 1957. We would be leaving from Long Beach, California.

Plans for Returning to Japan

Our year of furlough was coming to a close. All the preparations for returning to Japan kept us more than busy. Leo's responsibilities at the headquarters of the training center and mission's department put him in a place of close contact with the founder and director. We were becoming more and more disturbed by what we were seeing and hearing, yet we tried to close our eyes and ears. Surely it wasn't true.

We were within a week of our departure to return to Japan. The date was set and our trunks and crates were at the Long Beach dock. At this time the founder called Leo aside and confided in him. He told Leo he had been involved in an affair with a much younger woman over a period of several years. He had recently gone to Mexico for a divorce from his wife and marriage to the younger woman who was pregnant with his child. The founder had no intentions of resigning from his ministry. He was asking Leo if, even knowing the facts, he would continue to be a part of the mission in Japan.

Leo came home and shared with me what had been disclosed to him. We were stunned—absolutely stunned. What we didn't want to believe was true. It wasn't a matter to pray about. The decision was set in our hearts by the Word and Spirit of God. We resigned immediately. By this turn of events, we were forced to return to Japan without a stateside mission covering.

We knew our going back to Japan was God's will. There are times along life's way that we must cling to God alone. All around may seem as sinking sand, but we must be confident that we are standing on Christ the Solid Rock. This was one of those times.

Another Ocean Voyage

Toward the end of February 1957, Leo, Robby, and I boarded a Japanese freighter, the *American Maru,* at Long Beach Harbor. We had a first-class stateroom on the upper deck. Our excellent meals were with the officers of the ship, along with the other stateroom passengers.

The ship was a vessel used for transporting Japanese to Brazil. Many were immigrating there in those days. Some of the holds down below had been converted into accommodations for the immigrants. The food and living quarters were equivalent to the low fare they paid.

When we boarded the *American Maru,* the vessel was on a return trip to Japan with only a few passengers in the accommodations down below. For cargo the ship had taken on iron ore in Brazil and was loaded to the hilt.

Robby was now a very active one and a half year old. What he lacked in size, he made up for in energy. He required constant surveillance.

The following morning after our departure from land, we woke up to a churning ocean.

In spite of the excellent food offered us, no one felt like eating much. "But tomorrow it will be better," we told ourselves.

Tomorrow turned out to be worse. And the next day, and the next. The ship creaked and groaned under its heavy load. By the time we were about halfway across, the ocean was a heaving tumult of watery mountains and valleys. If you have never been there, don't ever wish to be.

This was ironic. On my first voyage across the ocean, I was disappointed because there were no whitecaps. Now we were experiencing an angry ocean of tumultuous mountains and valleys.

During the worst of the voyage, the ship would have to climb out of a valley onto a high mountain of water. The bow of the ship would go out over the top of the mountain until it slammed down on the other side. Then the stern with the rudder would be elevated out of water causing the ship to shake violently. Again, it was down into another valley where the bow of the ship would go under water until it could gain its equilibrium, only to have another watery mountain to climb.

There is a portion in Psalms that describes the ocean we were on:

> *"Their ships were tossed to the heavens and sank again to the depths..." Psalm 107: 26a (NLT)*

Our ship was constantly rocking and rolling and pitching. The only way we could sleep was to brace our backs against the wall of the bunk beds with our feet braced against the other side. In spite of the circumstances, God had kept us from the torment of fear.

On one occasion the pitching of the ship threw Robby off a low chair to the floor so forcefully, a deep gash was cut in his chin. It should have been stitched, but the doctor on board didn't have the equipment to do so. To this day a scar on his chin is a reminder of that voyage.

The captain finally decided it was too dangerous to even move. All the anchors were dropped. We sat there at the mercy of the violent ocean. We stayed anchored in mid-ocean for at least a day. When the violence had subsided a bit, the captain decided to move on, although it was still a very turbulent ocean we were struggling through.

What should have been an eighteen-day voyage to Japan, ended up taking twenty-three days.

1957-1969

Omuta

Our Second Missionary Term

The mountains and valleys of an angry ocean we encountered on our return to Japan were behind us. God had brought us safely through. Now we were back in Japan to continue the calling God had put upon us, a calling we cherished. We were trusting God to guide us in all the decisions that were to be made.

We were now missionaries without a mission covering. This was not what we would have chosen. It was brought upon us by a conviction we had deep in our hearts. Obedience to God's Word was never to be sacrificed for an easier pathway.

The first decision Leo and I needed to make was where we would go to pioneer a church. We wanted to return to Kyushu, but going back to Sendai did not seem to be an option.

Two things were deep in our hearts after the heartache we experienced at Sendai. Leo would never rely on an interpreter again. We would stay located at one place until a healthy church was established—"even if it takes fifteen years," we had said to each other.

My cousin Wilma had also married a fellow missionary, Dick Torres, a year after we were married. Dick and Wilma were pioneering a church in Minamata, Kumamoto Prefecture. They invited us to come and stay with them while we sought God for His direction where we should go to begin a new work.

A New Beginning—Omuta

When we were on the train going through Kyushu to the Torres', our attention was somehow drawn to the city of Omuta. It was a coal mining community in Fukuoka Prefecture. When the train stopped there for a few minutes, the loudspeakers on the station platform were resounding with the usual call of the name of the city, *"Oo-mu-TA, Oo-mu-TA!"*

At the Torres' Leo rose early every morning and walked on the hillside above their house praying earnestly for God's direction for us. As he prayed, *"Oo-mu-TA, Oo-mu-TA"* kept echoing in his head. Leo decided to go to Omuta to search it out. It was favorable. We felt God was guiding us to pioneer a church there, so by faith we began taking steps in that direction.

Leo and I made a prayer list of the things we desired to have in the place where we would live. Since pioneering a church in those days usually involved starting with services in your home, we wanted something adequate for that purpose. We needed a house. An apartment wouldn't do. We hoped for a fenced yard for Robby. The list went on.

Leo returned to Omuta a second time. This time he went to find the house we were praying about. Because the coal mines of Omuta provided employment, many people had crowded into that area. Any rental that came available was soon snatched up. There were very few houses in Omuta available for rent in those days. But God had gone before us and prepared the way. After four days of searching, Leo was able to rent the house that met all the needs we had put on the list.

We moved to Omuta in April 1957. Our few worldly possessions were still stored in a warehouse in Osaka. At our request the warehouse shipped our things to us by train. We used the first month in Omuta to get settled in our new location. All that month we were praying earnestly for God's guidance in every detail of establishing an indigenous, healthy church for His glory.

Arriving in Omuta, April 20, 1957. Robby was one and a half years.

Leo had in his heart, and often confessed it with words, that he wanted to "pioneer a church that would continue on until Jesus comes." Mistakes at Sendai had grieved us deeply. We didn't want to repeat those mistakes.

The Challenge of the Language *(by Leo)*

When we moved to Omuta, the city had a population of 220,000. The coal mines and their related industries offered employment for most of the working population of the city. Our challenge was to reach these people with the greatest news ever told—the gospel of Jesus Christ.

I desired to study the Japanese language effectively in order to communicate the gospel effectively. Never again did I want to be dependent upon an interpreter—I would communicate directly with the people.

With this in mind, I went to the Kawashiri Elementary School near our house to ask permission to attend classes with the school children. What better way to study the language than to learn it as the Japanese themselves learned it.

The school principal and the teachers graciously granted me permission to audit some classes. A special place was arranged for me at the back of the fifth grade classroom. This was the grade level I had chosen. In the schoolroom, my six-foot two-inch frame, blonde hair, and blue eyes drew much attention for the first few days. The children swarmed around me for my autograph. After a time my presence was just part of the fifth grade classroom.

I audited two classes each day—Japanese Language and Social Studies. I was hearing and feeling the Japanese language the children were learning. I continued to study this way for two years, through the fifth and sixth grades.

My attending classes at the elementary school created interest in the community. A local newspaper reporter came to take my picture and wrote up a story: "This six-foot two-inch, blue-eyed American is studying in the classroom with the small Japanese fifth graders." Even to this day, some forty-five years later, occasionally someone will tell me I was their classmate back in 1957-1959 at Kawashiri Elementary School.

Changes in Our Ministry Approach *(by Leo)*

In many ways our first four years in Japan had served as a learning experience for us. We had seen the powerful gospel of Christ transform lives. At the same time, we were introduced to the many difficulties of reaching a people who were of an entirely different culture than our own. Our respect for the Japanese continued to increase.

In our first four years in Japan, the emphasis of the mission we were with had been that we were to be mobile missionaries. They stressed that we were to follow the Apostle Paul's example; that Jesus is coming soon; that there is no time to stop to learn the language; or to plant yourselves in any one place. Just get an interpreter, pass out tracts, win souls, leave it all with the Japanese believers, and move on to the next city. There is too much to do to establish yourself in one place for long.

We observed this approach was not working to establish local churches. We found the Japanese people to be hesitant to follow you if they sensed you were only with them for a temporary time and then you would soon be gone. They looked for permanency and stability in you and your message.

When we came to Omuta, we came with changes in our approach toward our ministry. We wanted to establish a local church that would continue to grow until Jesus comes. We desired the church to be healthy and indigenous—a church filled with radiant Japanese Christians who would catch the vision of being a self-propagating, self-governing, self-supporting body of believers.

Two verses in particular became a part of our vision:

> *"You did not choose Me, but I chose you and appointed you that you should go and bear fruit, and that your fruit should remain..." (John 15:16).*

"And the things that you have heard from me among many
witnesses, commit these to faithful men who will be able
to teach others also" (II Timothy 2:2).

Therefore in pioneering a new church in Omuta, we determined to be there for the long term, no matter how long it would take.

Our First Meeting of the Omuta Church

Leo set Wednesday night, May 30, 1957, as the date for the first meeting of the church we were starting. Leo went throughout our neighborhood passing out flyers announcing that we would be starting church meetings in our home on May 30. He was meeting the neighborhood people and inviting them to come. We would also be singing church hymns. Everyone enjoys singing. Hymns are a wonderful proclamation of Who Christ is and the great salvation He has provided.

We purchased a small pump organ to aid in the music. The organ's keyboard was less than three feet long. I would have to be the organist. Music is not one of my giftings, so this was a challenge. I had a brush with piano lessons in my middle school years. After a year or so of lessons, the piano teacher kindly but truthfully informed Mama the money she was paying for my piano lessons was rather a waste. So there it ended.

Now years later, that little brush with piano lessons gave me the courage to do my best to learn to play the hymns on the organ. Since the people who would be coming to our meetings didn't know any hymns, we would teach them one song at a time. I practiced all week on that one song. The first song was *"What a Friend We Have in Jesus."* Before the next meeting, I had a whole week to practice one more song.

On the designated Wednesday night, that first meeting was attended by ten or fifteen people. They crowded into our *tatami* mat living room. Most of them were middle school and high school students who had primarily come out of curiosity. Whatever their motive, they were there and they would hear the gospel.

We had prayed earnestly for God to direct in every detail of pioneering this new church. We would do our best to do our part, and the Holy Spirit would do the work of salvation and changing lives.

Leo preached that night from Acts 9 about Saul of Tarsus who had an encounter with the risen Son of God. That encounter changed Saul into a steadfast believer in Jesus. Out of those ten or fifteen people in that first meeting, several continued to come regularly. Three of those first timers eventually were genuinely saved. Later the three went to Bible school and, in the years following, they themselves became ministers of the gospel. This was fruit that remains.

Omuta Church Begins to Develop *(by Leo)*

Starting with that first Wednesday night meeting, we continued with regular weekly services on Sunday mornings, Sunday evenings, and Wednesday evenings. We hung a sign on the fence in front of our rented house announcing these services.

A few people continued to come to each service. We envisioned that one day the church would be able to buy its own land and build its own church building. This would speak to the community that the church was here on a permanent basis.

From the very beginning, we taught the principle of tithing and giving offerings as instructed in the Scriptures. Some sighed in reluctance, "But we Japanese are poor. It's different for the Americans, because they are rich."

We replied, "God's way is tithing ten percent of what you have. The money given in obedience to this principle is the Lord's money.

We will save the tithes and offerings to buy land where we can build a church building." I remember the total offering for that first month amounted to less than $10.00. Though meager, it was a beginning.

As the small nucleus of believers grew, they began to catch the vision of tithing. In five or six years, the savings from the believers' offerings was sufficient to enable us to secure a bank loan and buy a piece of land for the church. The people were excited and so were we.

When the bank loan was paid off, we proceeded with plans to build facilities for the Omuta church. We stretched our faith for a building to accommodate about eighty people. That was a large church in those days.

The building was completed in March 1964, just seven years after our first meeting in 1957. There was great rejoicing in seeing what wonders God had performed, working in and through the Japanese believers. This was the beginning of what we set out to accomplish by putting our roots down in Omuta.

Our home and the Omuta church—built in 1964

Evangelistic Methods *(by Leo)*

We used various methods of evangelism to reach the people of Omuta with the gospel message. We went out to the streets and passed out tracts. We held street meetings at the main shopping area where each day hundreds of people walked by the many shops.

Each local area throughout the city had its own community hall for local gatherings. We would rent these community halls for two or three nights at a time and hold special evangelistic meetings for that local area. Those were the days before many people had a television in their own home. It was fairly easy to get people to attend the meetings at the community halls.

In about our third year of ministry in Omuta, a high school biology teacher attended one of those community hall meetings near his home. Nishiyama Sensei came each night and then began to attend our church services regularly. We learned that as a young man, he had been a Christian but had fallen away from God for a number of years. The preaching from the Bible and the singing of hymns stirred a spiritual slumber that had taken over within him. Nishiyama Sensei responded to the fresh working of the Holy Spirit in his heart.

Oota Sensei *(by Leo)*

Soon after coming to church, Nishiyama Sensei told us of the music teacher at his high school. Oota Sensei had a serious alcoholic problem. Each morning he would go to school under the influence of alcohol. His classes were bedlam.

I suggested we begin to pray that Oota Sensei would come to church and meet the Jesus Who could transform his life. A few weeks later, Oota Sensei attended one of the evening meetings in our home.

At the close of the service, I talked with Oota Sensei. I remember laying my hand on his shoulder in a friendly gesture. He told me later, that at the very moment I laid my hand on him, he felt a warm sensation go throughout his body. God touched him! By that touch from the Almighty God, Oota Sensei was instantly set free from alcoholism. Oota Sensei was overwhelmed by this wonderful God who had set him free from his terrible bondage. After that encounter Oota Sensei attended every church service and began to grow beautifully in his Christian life.

Oota Sensei radiant in Christ (early 1960s). Incidentally, Oota Sensei is standing on a footstool, as he was very short.

It wasn't long before Phyllis asked Oota Sensei if he would play the little pump organ for our services. Phyllis had done her best, but she was more than happy to have a replacement in the music. Oota Sensei seemed to have music flowing out of every cell in his body. In spite of his great accomplishments in music, he was a man of great humility. He made our little three-foot-long pump organ come alive.

In those early days of our ministry in Kyushu, there were, as yet, few people in any of the other churches with much musical ability. Oota Sensei's gift of music continued to bless our church and other fellowshipping churches for many years. He wrote several beautiful choruses that are still being sung today. After more than fifteen years of faithfully serving in the church with his music, Oota Sensei was suddenly taken from us to his reward in heaven. We greatly missed our beloved Oota Sensei.

Yamato San *(by Leo)*

A few months after Oota Sensei was saved, he and Nishiyama Sensei told me about another person at their school. Yamato San, who worked in the school office, was in great need of Christ's power of deliverance.

Before Oota Sensei was transformed by God's power, he and Yamato San would go out each evening to drink together. Now that Oota Sensei's life was completely changed, Yamato San lost his drinking partner. However, he continued his alcoholic habit that was destroying his health and his family.

Each month within a few days after payday, Yamato San would soon use up his monthly salary to satisfy his addiction to alcohol. This lifestyle continued to increase the terrible debt that he had accumulated.

Yamato San, with his wife and their four children, lived in poverty and despair. One day his wife strapped their youngest to her back, took their three-year-old by the hand, and headed for the railroad tracks. She had determined to plunge in front of an oncoming train and end it all. Fortunately, she didn't have the courage to carry out her plan and returned to their miserable home.

The doctor had told Yamato San, "If you don't stop drinking, you will die." Yamato San answered, "Fine, Doctor. I'd rather die than stop drinking." Drinking was Yamato San's temporary escape from his life of misery.

We heard about this sad story from Nishiyama Sensei and Oota Sensei. Again I said, "Let's pray for Yamato San to be saved and delivered." We prayed and waited for the opportunity to meet Yamato San and lead him to Christ.

That opportunity came a few months later when I visited the high school to talk with Nishiyama Sensei and Oota Sensei about some church business. They had been telling Yamato San about the American missionary who had come to their city to pioneer a church. They told him about the blessings of church. Of course, Yamato San knew only too well how Oota Sensei had been so totally transformed by his encounter with Christ.

While I was at the high school that day, the two teachers asked if I could take time to meet Yamato San. They brought him to the biology teacher's room. That science room was lined with shelves filled with jars of specimens of frogs, lizards, snakes, etc., all preserved in formaldehyde solution.

In this setting I began to talk with Yamato San. I read John 3:16 and explained to him of the love of God in the simplest way I knew how. Then I asked, "Do you understand?" Very straight forward he answered, "No, I don't". Indignation rose up inside me against the spiritual blindness that bound this man. I held my emotions at bay and calmly said, "Let's pray that God will reveal Himself to you."

We knelt on the floor of that high school science room. As I laid my hands on Yamato San and prayed for his deliverance, suddenly I was overwhelmed with the wonderful Presence of God. I knew God was touching Yamato San. However, it wasn't until the following Sunday when Nishiyama Sensei and Oota Sensei brought Yamato San to church that I learned what God had done for him.

This is the story Yamato San told us: He left the biology room as quickly as he could after I prayed for him. He said he was very uncomfortable in the presence of the American. He returned to his own room down the hall.

Yamato San told us how he reached out to take a cigarette. At that instant he heard a clear Voice speak, "From this day on, you will never smoke or drink again!" He was shocked! He looked around his room but saw no one. Thinking maybe he was just imagining this, he attempted to reach for his cigarettes a second time. Once again he heard the Voice clearly repeating the same words to him.

Yamato San recognized the Living God had spoken to him. His response was immediate. Taking his cigarettes down the hall to a friend, he simply said, "I don't need these any more." The friend laughed at him, but Yamato San knew the supernatural power of God had come into his life. An instant miracle had taken place. From that moment Yamato San never smoked, drank, or gambled again.

When he came to church with Nishiyama Sensei and Oota Sensei the following Sunday, Yamato San learned more about the Living God Who had touched him. On that Sunday, at the age of 43, he received Jesus as his Savior. Yamato San began reading the Bible and attended every church service. His wife joined him in attending church. She was amazed at the tremendous change that had come into her husband's life, and she, too, accepted Christ. The whole family came to church together.

As years passed some of Yamato's children had their own spiritual encounter with Christ and became joyful Christians. The

Yamato family have been pillars in our church for many years. Now at this writing, some forty-four years after Yamato San's life was transformed, there are four generations of the Yamato family in our church.

Oota Sensei's and Yamato San's outstanding deliverances took place in the early years of our ministry in Omuta. Again we rejoiced to see fruit that remains.

Yamato San and his wife a number of years after they were transformed from poverty and devastation to rejoicing in Christ's salvation

Our Family Salvation Began with My Father

By Mikio Yamato—Translated by Leo Kaylor

Mikio Yamato

My father's life was filled with endless dissipation. With no concern for the family, he carelessly used his meager salary on himself—drinking, smoking, and gambling. My mother suffered great hardship trying to sustain the family.

During my teenage years, I hated my father and determined never to become like him. When my father was not at home, our family had fun together. But as soon as he came home, we all fell silent and darkness would cover us.

One day Leo Kaylor Sensei went to the public high school to see Oota Sensei, the Christian music teacher. Oota Sensei invited my father, who also worked at the same high school, to meet Kaylor Sensei and hear about Christ.

That very day my father heard God speak to him. He heard a Voice as though it were audible. "From this day on, you will never smoke or drink again!" My father believed in the Lord, and his life was instantaneously changed and delivered from his addiction to *sake* (Japanese rice wine) and tobacco.

My father was transformed from a life of wretchedness to a full life of joy. Now he was smiling all day long and rejoicing by saying, "Hallelujah! Hallelujah!" My mother and sisters accompanied him to Kaylor Sensei's church.

But as for me, I saw the way my father had made such a sudden change without any apologies for all the unhappiness he had caused the family. Now that he was intent on going to church, I thought to myself, "How self-centered!" I hated him that much more.

My father also insisted that I go to church with the family. I did go, but only begrudgingly. Since church was always on Sundays, I could not go to watch my favorite baseball games. I determined not to go to church again.

Since I could not respect my father or have any fun at home, I decided I would leave. I was seventeen. I would go to work on my own, make money, and prove my success. I went to Osaka, which was a long distance away, and got a job.

To me, without money, there was no happiness or fulfillment of dreams. I did not need to trust in God to live a successful life. I determined I would not live a life like my father. But just like the Japanese proverb says, "The child of a frog is a frog," or, in other words, "Like father, like son." Very soon I was living the same kind of life I had seen my father live.

Regardless of my feelings toward my father, I still wanted to go back home whenever I had vacation time. But, as always, my father would say, "You must go to church!"

I would react against this, "I didn't come home just to go to church." He would sternly reply, "Then go on back to Osaka!" It was tit-for-tat. I would come home only to run away again. It was my mother who became the go-between for my father and me.

One summer when I went home, I learned the church's summer conference was at the Unzen Resort across Ariake Bay. My whole family was preparing to go. Since no one would be at home to prepare meals, I went along with the family. This way I would have good food, escape the summer heat, and enjoy sightseeing.

Totally contrary to my personal desire, I got stuck in the conference meetings. A friend from school days, whom I respected and who was now a Bible school student, compelled me to stay in the meetings.

Finally, it was the last day of the conference. That's when God got hold of me! It was during the prayer time at the very end. I casually thought it wouldn't hurt for me to join in just a bit, so I began to pray along with everyone else. I did as I saw everyone else doing. I stood up, raised my hands, and started saying, "Hallelujah."

Suddenly, my whole body began to shake. I was puzzled about what was happening to me. I looked around, but no one else was shaking. It was only me. I was embarrassed. I wanted to stop the shaking, but I couldn't, not even by holding my knees tightly with my hands.

I said to myself, "God must be here, and if I don't believe, something dreadful might happen to me."

The conference ended, but I didn't tell anyone about my strange experience. I just kept it to myself and returned to my work in Osaka. However, in my heart, I determined to find a church to attend.

I located a church and began attending the services. I received salvation through the cross of Jesus Christ; my whole life of sins was forgiven. I was filled with joy and hope, and my value system about life was changed.

During one meeting I had a vision. I saw my life of sins all written out before me. I could not deny a single sin and I collapsed under the heavy weight of them. I wept profusely, crying, "O Jesus! Help me!"

At that instant I saw a Lamb being slain and its blood flowed out and covered all my sins. Nothing was left to be seen of them. I received the wonderful assurance that everything was forgiven.

> *"What happiness for those whose guilt has been forgiven! What joys when sins are covered over! What relief for those who have confessed their sins and God has cleared their record" Psalms 32:1, 2. (LB)*

I am so grateful that I am what I am today because Kaylor Sensei and his wife came to share the gospel. First of all my father was saved, then my mother, then all of us four children.

1969-1973
Yakushima and Kagoshima

Yakushima

Yakushima is one of Japan's many semi-tropical islands in the East China Sea. It is a small, round, very mountainous island about one hundred miles directly south of Kagoshima City. Its beautiful, rugged mountains are filled with giant cedar trees. Many are estimated to be several thousand years old. The number of deer and of monkeys on the island are said to exceed the population of the people.

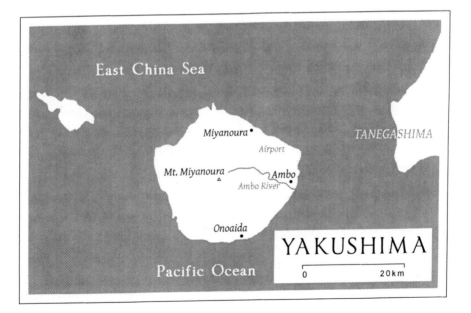

Yakushima has become a popular tourist attraction. The picturesque mountains of great beauty, the ancient cedar trees, the sandy beaches on which sea turtles return year after year to lay their eggs, the brilliant hibiscus flowers that bloom almost year around are among its numerous attractions. In 1993 Yakushima was given the prized designation of being a World Natural Heritage Site, granted by the United Nations.

In recent years the population of Yakushima has dwindled to about 13,000. In spite of its beauty and treasures, there is little to hold its young people on the island.

The Gospel Reaches Yakushima

A young missionary went to the isolated island of Yakushima in 1957 to search out the possibilities of pioneering a church there. If all went well, he would later bring his wife and small daughter and together they would begin their missionary career on the island.

Yakushima at that time had a population of about 30,000. It was virgin territory for the work of the gospel. The young missionary, with great dedication to God's call on his life, was hoping to enter this very challenging isolated mission field.

Back in those days, the trip to Yakushima by a small ferryboat took about eight hours from Kagoshima. It was an island-hopping voyage. Often the sea was turbulent, which meant some very miserable hours of being relentlessly tossed to and fro on board the small vessel.

The young missionary's trip to Yakushima in 1957 turned out to be the stomach-wrenching kind on a rough sea. It left the missionary "pale as a ghost and green at the gills," as he sometimes described it.

Because of his hours of such sufferings to reach the small island, the missionary had a change of mind en-route. He made the decision he would just return to Kagoshima where he had embarked.

He would look elsewhere for a place to minister the gospel other than this small, hard-to-get-to island.

That day in 1957, with the very sick missionary on board, the little ferry finally anchored a short distance from the Yakushima shore at the town of Ambo. In those days there was no port. A small barge-like boat went out from the shore to the anchored ferry to meet the passengers and their baggage. When the barge came to the ferry's side, the heaving ocean tossed the ferry upward while the barge was dropped downward. Then the turbulent waves would send the ferry down and the barge up.

It was a nerve-wracking experience to choose the right moment to leap from the ferry's deck into the pitching barge. The missionary had no intention of making the leap as he had already changed his mind about going ashore on this small island. But God had other plans! As the missionary stood on the heaving deck, his bags were thrown into the barge. He now had no choice but to follow them ashore.

On shore someone approached the foreigner to help him with his bags. The dejected missionary didn't know the language. He pulled out a piece of paper from his shirt pocket that he had prepared. It was a written explanation in Japanese of who he was and what his intentions were—a missionary to teach islanders about Christ and His salvation.

The kind man who came to help carry his bags read the note. He then threw his hands heavenward and in faltering English he exclaimed, "Hallelujah! I am Christian!" The man was Yoshikazu Takeshita, whom God had arranged to be there on shore that day when His beloved, weary servant arrived.

The missionary, with his wife and small daughter, returned to Yakushima the following year, 1958. They spent several very profitable years ministering the gospel on the island. A church was established and also a Christian kindergarten was started in Onoaida on the south side of the island. Takeshita San and his wife worked side by side with the missionary.

*Yoshikazu Takeshita and his wife as they are today. They have had a
ministry in Yakushima for over forty years.*

Leo talking to the kindergarten children

Onoaida Christian Kindergarten

Onoaida Christian Kindergarten in Yakushima had its beginning in 1960. It was birthed out of a burden in the pioneer missionary's heart to reach the island with the gospel message in every way possible.

Those first kindergarten classes were held in the missionary's home with only a few children attending. Takeshita San's wife was one of the teachers.

From that humble beginning, an excellent Christian kindergarten has been established by the dedication and persistence of Takeshita Sensei and his wife. In more recent years, their daughter Mamiko joined them in ministering to the children.

One little boy who was in the first class of children to graduate from the kindergarten became a man of public influence. He is now the elected official who represents Yakushima in the Kagoshima prefectural government. For the kindergarten's special events, he sends a congratulatory telegram as from "a member of the first graduating class of the kindergarten."

Some years ago the Takeshitas asked Leo to be the honorary principal (*Encho Sensei*) of the kindergarten. Filling this position Leo travels to the island several times a year for their special events. It is a pleasure for me to go with Leo on those trips. The children love for *Encho Sensei* to come. They get a thrill putting their little hands into his big hand for a friendly handshake.

After more than forty years, over 2,500 children have graduated from the kindergarten. Many of those children are now adults and scattered all over Japan. The Word of God that was planted in their hearts during their young and tender years can bring forth eternal life as the Holy Spirit blows upon it. We are praying it shall be so.

Hidaka Sensei

Akifumi Hidaka was saved, healed, and called into the ministry as a result of the missionary's very fruitful work in Yakushima. Some of God's most precious servants are tucked away where others don't often see them. Hidaka Sensei is one such servant.

Hidaka Sensei seldom gives the slightest hint of the hard blows life had dealt him. If he does make mention of it, he tells it with a smile and with gestures that emphasize the smile.

At birth in 1939, Akifumi San was laid aside as dead. But his grandmother noticed a slight flicker of life and managed to revive his tiny body. From birth his right arm and leg did not function properly and this left him disabled. When he started school, the teachers forced him to use his right hand, although he had better use of his left hand. This frustrated him terribly.

When Akifumi San was in the first grade, his father passed away with tuberculosis. Death tormented his young mind. By the time he was in the fourth grade, his grandfather, mother, and brother also died of tuberculosis. Akifumi San's endearing grandmother then cared for him.

At seventeen Akifumi San went to the neighboring island of Tanegashima to learn the trade of shoe repair. This was very difficult for him because of his disability. Akifumi San became weakened by tuberculosis and asthma. When he was twenty, he was sent back to his home in Yakushima to die. Man had, again, laid Akifumi San aside as hopeless.

God had arranged that the missionary who went to Yakushima in 1958, lived for a time in Akifumi San's grandmother's home. When Akifumi San returned from Tanegashima to his grandmother's, he met the missionary. Akifumi San was very moved by the story of Christ's salvation that the missionary told him. He accepted Jesus as his Savior and was baptized. During the next six months, instead of dying, health began to reign in his body. Akifumi San realized God had healed him.

Akifumi San dedicated his life to God and eventually went to Bible school to prepare for the ministry. He was now called by the title of Hidaka Sensei. After a few years God gave him a wonderful wife. From 1967, together with his wife, they pastored their church in the town of Miyanoura on the northeast side of Yakushima. Hidaka Sensei and his wife birthed ministry in the hearts of others. Among them were three young ladies who became pastors' wives. They now have growing churches in other places in Japan.

Many other Christians are scattered throughout Japan who are fruit from Hidaka Sensei's faithful ministry.

Sixteen years into their pastoring, Hidaka Sensei's wife was taken from him after a year of illness. He was left with five young children ranging in ages from thirteen to less than two years. Now, besides pastoring his church, he had to fill the roles of both father and mother. Hidaka Sensei got a job to support his family, but faithfully continued Sunday morning worship in his church. His five children are now grown and away from home.

Hidaka Sensei tells that when he was young, he would always come in last in any race with his classmates, due to his physical disability. Now at age sixty-five, Hidaka Sensei laughingly claims that if they had a race, he could outrun any of his former classmates with all their aches and pains and infirmities!

*Hidaka Sensei in front of his church where
he has served faithfully for many years*

Our Move to Yakushima

The missionary who had pioneered the work on Yakushima had done an amazing job. However, about seven years later, it became necessary for him and his family to leave the island because of his wife's health. At that time he asked Leo if he would oversee the Yakushima work.

By 1969 the Omuta church was doing well under the leadership of a young man who was saved in our ministry. He had dedicated his life to God, had gone to Bible school, and then returned to our church. After a few years of working under Leo, the young man appeared capable of carrying the leadership of the Omuta church. Therefore, Leo set him in as pastor.

The need for leadership in Yakushima was pulling at our hearts. There was no one to send, so we decided to go ourselves for a period of time. We made the move from Omuta to Yakushima the summer of 1969.

A church and a Christian kindergarten had been established in the village of Onoaida on the south side of the island. In Ambo on the east side, a two-story building had been built. Another Christian kindergarten was operating on the first floor of those facilities by the time we arrived on the island. The second floor of the Ambo building sufficed for living quarters for our family.

Takeshita Sensei and his wife who lived in Onoaida did a great job carrying on the responsibilities of the kindergartens after the missionary left. Even though they had no Bible school training, they were also doing their best with the church services in Onoaida. At the same time, Takeshita Sensei continued in full-time employment. After we arrived Leo ministered in the Onoaida church on Sunday mornings.

By the time we moved to Yakushima in 1969, traveling to the island had changed considerably since the pioneer missionary's first trip in 1957. A large, beautiful ferry now transported both people and cars as it plied daily between Kagoshima and Yakushima. It now took only four hours to reach the island on the new vessel. An airport was also built on the island. A thirty-minute plane ride could now take the place of long hours by ferry.

Life on the Island

When we moved to Yakushima, we had four children. Rob was fourteen; Steven, ten; Nathan, nine; and Joyce, six. Their schooling was no problem since we were homeschooling. We just provided desks for all of them in our new place of living and continued with their education. It all worked smoothly, as far as homeschooling can be smooth!

Our family when we lived on Yakushima.
Left to right, Steven, Nathan, Rob, Joyce.

Yakushima was a paradise of beautiful surroundings. We had the mountains to hike in, or the beach with its varied enchantments. We discovered there were many beautiful seashells on some of the rocky shores. At one point we became intrigued with shells as tiny as a grain of sand, and yet so perfect in many shapes and colors. What the naked eye couldn't find, a magnifying glass helped us in our searching.

We learned we couldn't find whole shells on sandy shores. Even big shells would be half worn away from the "sanding" they constantly received. Oh, the beauty of some of those sandy beaches—clean, white sand with blue, blue water. If it had been a populated area, the beaches would have been filled with beach goers. The islanders had no time for relaxing in the sand and sun. We usually had the whole beach to ourselves on Mondays, which was our family day.

Steven, Nathan, and Joyce were baptized at the mouth of the Ambo River. The township of Ambo is in the background.

The Ambo River was only a skip and a jump from the building where we lived. In the summertime, the children practically lived in their swimsuits. Even before breakfast they would often head for the river and take a cool, refreshing dip. Because Yakushima is semi-tropical, daytime temperatures were very hot in the summer. The river was a wonderful place to cool off. Ocean breezes and the mountains rising high above the island's shoreline where the people lived helped the nights to be comfortably cool.

The Unexpected

We had lived on Yakushima Island less than a year when, in the early months of 1970, we learned we were expecting our fifth child. Leo and I welcomed the surprise with joy. The baby would be due in August.

By now our youngest, Joyce, was seven. We considered children a blessing from God and took great pleasure in them. We were looking forward to another blessing.

I was approaching the fourth month of the pregnancy when I experienced some disturbing symptoms. We contacted the island doctor and he confirmed a miscarriage was imminent. The doctor suggested I enter his hospital for complete bed rest. His hospital was a small facility with limited equipment. I was admitted into one of the few rooms. It didn't appear the cleaning lady had been on duty for a while.

This predicament was extremely difficult for me. Lying in the hospital and doing nothing, while the family needed my help at home, caused me much agony of mind. But we did want to protect the life of our baby.

Leo and Rob made the family meals, did the family laundry, and everything else to keep the household running. Besides all of that, they also had to bring my meals as the "hospital" provided none.

Shortly after I was admitted, the doctor came into my room with his little pet monkey—a real, live one with dancing, shining eyes! I'm sure the doctor's intention was to cheer me up. He set the little monkey on my bed and asked if I would like for it to keep me company for awhile. Then he left. My mind raced. Cats and monkeys are known as disease-carrying animals, so I had heard. Later, I was relieved when the doctor came back and retrieved his little pet.

I endured several miserable days in the hospital. Being separated from the family was indeed miserable, even though they valiantly carried on without any complaints. We asked if I could observe bed rest at home. The doctor gave his permission. In his opinion the miscarriage hadn't taken place.

With the doctor's orders, even though he gave no further examinations, I stayed in bed rest for almost two months. I sometimes wondered, though, if our baby were still safely tucked away in the womb. I discerned there were no flutterings of a little life, and there didn't seem to be any enlargement of my abdomen.

I became impatient after a time and decided I could surely help out with the family work. With Leo's permission I made the effort to do some of the laundry. In a short time, what little energy I had escaped from my body, and I collapsed on the sofa finding it difficult just to breathe. It was a frightening experience. So back to bed rest it was.

After about two months, I gained strength enough to make the four-hour ferry trip to Kagoshima for an examination in the large, well-equipped University Hospital. The doctor there informed us a miscarriage had indeed taken place early on. The bed rest had given my body the time it needed to repair itself. We were told everything was in a healthy state.

Leo and I were disappointed to have lost our baby. At the same time, we were relieved to be out of the uncertainty about it. God spared us of grief and sorrow. This incident has caused me to reflect back on Daddy's dream about the empty suitcase labeled "Sorrows."

Later God did bless Leo and me with two more children. Joel was born January 1972, and Melodee, October 1973.

A Time to Seek God Afresh *(by Leo)*

Our time spent living on the isolated island of Yakushima gave me plenty of opportunity to read and re-read God's Word. I had a great desire to grasp more of God. During this time of intense study of the Scriptures, God revealed some very precious truths to my heart.

In those days of being refreshed in God's Word, we were introduced to the worship tapes sent out by Bible Temple in Portland, Oregon. Dick Iverson was the pastor.

As those worship tapes reached us in far away Yakushima, our hungry hearts were fed and nourished by the sound of congregational praise and worship. Pastor Iverson's preaching of the Word was like rivers of living water that brought refreshing to our spirits.

We made plans to travel to the U.S. for a short three months during the summer of 1971. We visited Bible Temple in Portland and met Pastor Dick Iverson. We saw for ourselves how Bible Temple was being blessed by an outpouring of the Holy Spirit. We were thrilled to find a church that was moving in the spirit of revival along the very same principles that God had been revealing to my own heart.

Returning to Japan August 1971, we now moved our family from Yakushima to Kagoshima. During our time in Kagoshima, Joel David was born January 9, 1972.

1973-1974

Under Pastor Iverson's Ministry

Pastor Iverson Ministers in Japan *(by Leo)*

In February 1973 Pastor Dick Iverson was invited to come to Japan to minister at the annual Japan Pentecostal Ministers' Conference. This conference was a gathering of Pentecostal and Charismatic pastors from all over the nation who were desirous for revival in Japan.

Pastor Iverson shared truths on "The Importance and Value of the Local Church," "The Church and End-Time Revival," and "Restoration of the Tabernacle of David Worship." His messages took root in the hearts of many pastors, giving them a new faith and vision for their churches.

During the years that followed, Pastor Iverson's ministry and the influence of Bible Temple have continued to greatly impact churches throughout Japan. This also opened the door for Japanese young people from the churches in Japan to attend Portland Bible College. This college was founded by Pastor Iverson under the local church of Bible Temple (now City Bible Church). Through the years several hundred Japanese young people have attended the college and have since returned to find fruitful ministry in churches across Japan.

A Year of Refreshing

When Pastor Iverson came to Japan in February 1973, he was also scheduled to minister in several Kyushu churches before the conference. Leo traveled with him as his interpreter. This gave Leo the privilege of spending quality time with Pastor Iverson.

We were in a period of transition in our ministry, and we shared with Pastor Iverson our need for a refreshing. Pastor Iverson invited us to come and spend some time in Bible Temple. Therefore, at his kind invitation, we took our family to Portland, Oregon, in June 1973 for one year.

All of our family greatly benefited from the blessings of Bible Temple that year. We were refreshed in their joyful praise and worship. Leo was asked to teach several courses at Portland Bible College, which was a part of Bible Temple. He also benefited from attending other classes at the college.

Rob, our eldest, had completed his high school studies through homeschool. He enrolled in Portland Bible College that fall. Steven, first year of high school; Nathan, eighth grade; and Joyce, sixth grade, all enrolled in Portland public schools. With the three children in public schools, the blessings of homeschooling were occasionally emphasized to us. Contending with humanism as taught by some of the teachers was something we never had to deal with in teaching our own children.

One day Steven came home from high school and told us, "There was a rumble at school today." Steven had to explain to us that a "rumble" was a time when angry students from a different school enter the school to fight and make havoc. We learned later it wasn't unusual for a rumble to happen. It can be a dangerous situation. Homeschooling is free from such happenings.

During that year in Bible Temple, we became members of the church, and they became our spiritual covering for our ministry in Japan. We had desired to have such a covering for many years.

Cherished friendships were created during that year. Our acquaintance with Kevin and Joyce Conner was among those very special friendships. Leo had the privilege of sitting under the teaching of Kevin Conner, who became like a "father in the faith" to him. His invaluable teaching confirmed and added volumes to some of the things Leo had searched out on his own during our time living on the island of Yakushima.

Things We Learned at Bible Temple *(by Leo)*

The year we spent in Portland at Bible Temple (1973-1974) was filled with many blessings. We were immersed in the many aspects of a large, healthy church that was flowing in the spirit of revival.

Some of what we learned and experienced can be summed up as follows:

1. We experienced the Presence of God in the flow of worship.

2. The truths concerning the establishing and growth of the healthy, local church were strengthened in our hearts.

3. We experienced being a part of the eldership and team ministry in the local church.

4. We were challenged afresh with the desire to teach and train workers for the harvest.

5. We learned more about the truths of the restoration of the church. The church began on the Day of Pentecost with great power and anointing of the Holy Spirit. However, the church went through a period of decline through the Middle Ages. Since the days of Martin Luther, God has been in the process of restoring the church to her former glory and power. The church of the end-time will reach God's intended eternal purpose to take the gospel of the Kingdom into all the world.

6. The restoration of the family. If the church is to be healthy, individual families must be healthy.

7. We learned about the importance of the five-fold ministry as listed in Ephesians 4:11. The work of the apostle, prophet, evangelist, pastor, and teacher is necessary to see the church fully equipped.

These truths, and much more, filled our hearts during that year at Bible Temple.

Times of Joy and Times of Sadness

When Leo and I, and our five children arrived in the U.S. the summer of 1973, I was very large with the pregnancy of our sixth child. In those days you didn't know if your baby was a boy or girl until it was born. Since we already had four boys and one girl, it was obvious which we were wishing for. Melodee Ruth made her appearance October 4, 1973. Six wonderful children now filled our quiver. Each of our children has brought much joy to Leo and me.

Life is filled with many joyful times. But there are also times of sadness we are all eventually called upon to walk through.

In the spring of 1974, Mama was diagnosed as having cancer. By the time it was discovered, it had spread throughout her body. The doctor estimated she had six months to live. We were all stunned. Yet, we needed to hold our heads high for Daddy's sake, for everyone else's sake, for our own sake.

Throughout my childhood I was a timid, skinny, little girl whom few people thought would make much in life. Mama was my encourager. There were those adolescent years with the usual concerns of trying to measure up to others. When I expressed those concerns to Mama, she would always tell me, "It's okay. Don't let those things concern you. You are fine just the way you are." What a treasure through all of my growing up days to have such an encourager as Mama was to me.

Now we were faced with the possibility that Mama may not be with us much longer. It was difficult to comprehend. However, we didn't just back off and wait for the worst.

We contended for God's healing power in Mama's body.

In the fall of 1974, Leo and I, along with five of our children, were scheduled to return to Japan. Rob was enrolled in Portland Bible College and therefore would not be returning with us. We decided that remaining in the U.S. wouldn't help the situation of Mama's sickness. Daddy and Mama both desired for us to go back to the land of our calling. So we returned to Japan in September.

Back in Japan word from Daddy through letters and telephone calls confirmed that Mama was weakening. In February 1975 we got a letter from Daddy saying the doctor gave Mama about two more weeks to live. I wished I could hurry home. But I didn't want to leave Leo with the care of five children, two of them very young. February 24 we got the phone call, "Mama is with Jesus."

Mama and Daddy—treasures to us four children

Zella, Paul, me, Sam (Picture taken in 1990)

As it turned out, not being there to walk through Mama's departure made it difficult for me to really comprehend that she was gone. I found myself, long afterwards, avoiding pictures of Mama because of the pain it would cause. A number of years later, I wrote a poem in memory of Mama. It became the bridge of healing I needed.

Thank You, Dear Mama

Dear Mama, your love is so real in my heart,
Even though you're gone, it will never depart.
Loving memories come flooding across the way,
As though they were but yesterday.

That humble little house with the howling stair,
Was home sweet home because you were there.
Our happy little home nestled deep in those hills,
Filled with love and contentment and quite a few thrills.

What could be more thrilling on Christmas morn,
There in the kitchen where it was nice and warm,
Than to look in my stocking and find a balloon there,
That had been purchased and placed with your loving care.

Or pulling our sleds to the top of the hill,
Sledding in the snow and taking a spill.

Or riding the bike you had purchased for us three;
Yes, life with contentment was happy and free.

In summertime Hay after the heat of the day,
You'd go to your garden to water and spray.
Then we three would run to the old garden gate,
And for a freshly plucked carrot we would patiently wait.

You'd wash them off good with the long garden hose,
Through which fresh spring water did water the rows.
You'd hand us each one as you had always done;
Then off to our play we would happily run.

Snapper would follow us as we each ate our prize,
With her ears perked up and a sparkle in her eyes.

My thoughts go back to our school days at Hay.
Every so often we would have a school play.
Mothers would gather in the old school gym,
(But it wasn't so old thinking way back then.)

Out on the stage as we each took our place,
I'd search the crowd for your smiling face.
Others who gathered were just images there,
But you stood out with love, warmth, and care.

You'd smile at me, and it made me so proud,
That you were my mama out there in the crowd.

When we were up from our nap and ready for play,
Sometimes you had something you wanted to say.
"You must pull all these weeds from here to here."
How I hated that job of yesteryear.

And memory reminds me of another situation--
All the flies in the house for the summer duration.
We'd swat those flies for hours unnumbered,
But our pay wasn't bad for a penny a hundred.

And now I look back and those memories I treasure,
That you taught us to work and that with good measure.

In modesty and virtue, Mama, you did excel,
And the importance of these you taught us so well.
Your standards became mine through all of my days,
And they guided me safely through life's worldly maze.

Thank you, dear Mama, for your love you have given;
It will always warm our hearts, though you've gone on to heaven.

Dedicated to you, Daddy, in honor of Mama
who has gone on ahead of us.

February 1994

Our Children

We are Blessed with Six

Leo and I are blessed with six wonderful children. Robert Leo, our first, was born August 23, 1955. He was three and a half years old when Steven Everett blessed our home January 1, 1959. A year and two months later on March 10, 1960, Nathan Jeremy joined us. Being so close in age, Steven and Nathan were inseparable all their growing up days, whether it was in their play or in their conflicts.

Lacy, pink dresses came into our home for the first time when Joyce LaRae was born October 25, 1962. Our feminine little girl was always a ray of sunshine in our family. Over nine years later, Joel David was born January 9, 1972. When Joel was a few months old, I made a discovery. Leo has no middle name, only the initial "J." One day I happened to realize Leo's name spelled backward came out "Joel." Interesting!

Our family of six children was completed when Melodee Ruth was born October 4, 1973. Melodee was another sweet, feminine touch we all needed. Nonetheless, at an early age, Joel found Melodee wasn't an easy, little, feminine push over. In his dealings with her, he learned using a bit of psychology produced better results than forced manpower!

God loves variety and our family is just that. Each of the children has his or her own rich personality and characteristics God gave them. Like any other household, stirring all these differences together doesn't always come out with peace and harmony—peace and harmony have to be worked into the household.

From the time the children were very small, we set aside Monday as family day. Our activities for that day revolved around the children. As Monday approached the question was often asked, "Daddy, what are we going to do on Fun Day?"

We endeavored from the beginning to make missionary life a happy experience for our children. God planted in Leo and me the desire to make our children our first responsibility of ministry. With that in its proper place, we could guide the children to feel a part with us in our church ministry.

Schooling for Our Children

We were in the U.S. for a two-year furlough when Robby, as we called him in his younger years, was in the first and second grades. During that two-year period, Joyce was born. We returned to Japan in 1963 with our four children to continue our ministry in Omuta.

One of the big hurdles for missionaries is schooling for their children. Now we were face to face with that hurdle. We had heard so many sad stories of missionaries sending their children away to boarding schools, but we didn't want our children to become one of those sad stories. Leo and I knew God had called us to be missionaries in Japan. We considered our children to be part of that calling during their growing-up years.

After considering all the options for the children's education, we decided on homeschooling. Back in those days, homeschooling was not often considered an option. Nonetheless, Leo and I decided this is the way we would go. We were trusting God to guide us in this very important decision.

We had been told there was a correspondence school in the U.S. through which we could get all the materials for homeschooling. We were stepping into a great unknown when we ordered the materials for Robby's third grade subjects.

Rob at his homeschool studies. Bedrooms were also classrooms.

Helping Steven with some of his studies

Joel at the wall of ABCs

I wish I could say it flowed easily—it didn't. The main difficulty was the stress I felt in carrying the responsibility of educating our own children. The stress and frustration I had allowed in my emotions put me under a heavy burden.

One day I came to the realization that because of my fears and frustrations, the schooling was on top of me and was relentlessly commanding me. I should be commanding the schooling. I resolved to turn the tables around. From that day the situation changed. I learned I had to take it one day at a time. If I succeeded today, that was enough—tomorrow I would face tomorrow's challenges.

In the children's younger years, it was always a challenge to keep them concentrating on their studies. That is a normal part of homeschooling. But as the children grew older, they each applied themselves diligently to their studies. This was an important element that helped our homeschooling to succeed. I did the teaching, the children diligently studied, and Leo continually offered his encouragement. We were all in it together.

When we had special evangelistic meetings or other special church events, we would close the school books. The children worked side-by-side with us passing out tracts, working at the street meetings, and helping set up tent meetings. They enjoyed being considered a part of our ministry.

There can be a tendency for parents who choose homeschooling to allow the desire to excel push them beyond just succeeding. Because of the many difficulties that accompany homeschooling, the desire to excel can become strife. The strife to excel is one of the things in life that never says, "It is enough!"

Now, many years later, I can look back again at God's gracious Hand upon us through the homeschooling part of our missionary life. All six of our children continued in homeschooling through high school. My goal was to succeed with the homeschooling. And I can sincerely say it was by His grace we did succeed.

1974-1987
We Return to Omuta

Challenges

The man whom Leo had set in as pastor of the Omuta church in 1969 continued pastoring with noticeable success. Over a period of years, his ministry brought the church into spiritual and numerical growth that was encouraging to observe.

When we returned to Japan in the fall of 1974, the Omuta pastor invited us to return to Omuta and work with him in the church. A number of promising young men had dedicated themselves to be trained for the ministry. Leo was asked to head up a Bible school training program in the Omuta church.

On our return to Omuta, our first challenge was finding a house large enough to accommodate our family of seven. It was a bigger challenge than we had anticipated. Most rentals were very small and impossible for our family to squeeze into. We searched for a suitable rental for several months with no success.

In the meantime the Omuta church facilities became our home. We lived out of our suitcases, and slept in the church classrooms. It was a difficult time with many challenges.

During those difficult months living in the church classrooms, Joel, almost three, became very ill with whooping cough. It was spreading among the children in the church. Joel's sickness became a real concern to us as the frightening cough got worse. He was thin and weak. I still shudder when I remember how it tore at my heart to see him try to cram his little fist into his throat as he struggled for breath.

Leo and I fasted and prayed for Joel. We took him to a doctor and he was given a shot. The sickness was broken and Joel recovered quickly. Whether the healing comes through fasting and prayer or through doctors and medicine, our faith is in the Great Healer. We had much praise in our hearts for Joel's healing.

A House for Us

In spite of the very difficult living conditions we were in, we were confident that God was orchestrating His plan in the situation. A realtor had shown us an appealing house that was still under construction. It was a large house, in Japanese standards, that would meet our needs, but it was for sale. We had never considered buying a house as we didn't have the finances to do so. But it seemed God was nudging us to step out in faith and believe for what seemed to be the impossible.

We felt God's gracious Hand upon us and obeyed His nudging. We secured some promises of loans in the U.S. that would enable us to make the down payment. With this in place, we signed the contract and paid the earnest money that was required. The deadline for the down payment was set for a few weeks hence.

The transfer of the dollars from the U.S. bank to our bank in Omuta took more time than we had expected. Over a period of weeks before the deadline of the down payment was due, Leo had made several treks to the bank to see if the money had come in. Each time he was told, "No money from America has arrived for you." If we missed the deadline, the deal was off and the earnest money we had paid would be lost. We became uneasy due to the delay of the money transfer.

The deadline day arrived. Leo went back to the bank that day with some anxiety in his heart, but we also had confidence that

God had led us to take this step of faith in signing the contract for the house. Leo pushed aside those feelings of anxiety and went boldly into the bank. At the counter he was told, "No, Mr. Kaylor. No money from America has arrived for you."

Leo was in the bank to do business—God's business. He quickly thought of a plan. Knowing there was money coming in, perhaps he could get a short term loan for a few days from the bank for the amount we needed today. His request was an unwelcome one and was flatly refused. So Leo took a seat in the waiting area and waited. He was confident that God was at work. We needed the money now.

A bank is not a place where you linger once you have finished your business. You are expected to leave. Leo's sitting there brought strange looks from the clerks. He felt as if he were under suspicion.

After some time Leo became uneasy to just sit there any longer, so he stood and turned to walk out of the bank. Just then a clerk from the far end of the bank came hurrying forward and called, "Mr. Kaylor!" Leo returned to the counter and was told, "Ten thousand dollars has just arrived from America for you!" In an instant the demeanor of all the bank clerks changed. Suddenly Leo became an honored and respected customer! We again basked in the providential Hand of our God that was upon us and rejoiced at His impeccable timing!

In February 1975 our family moved into our wonderful house. All these many years since, it has been a haven of rest for us.

Days of Blessing

The Omuta church continued to do very well. The pastor's presentation of salvation through Christ and of dedicating one's life to God was very effective. He was continuing to lead the growing congregation into spiritual blessings.

Leo taught a class for adults Sunday mornings before worship service. He was systematically teaching a series on church life principles. These principles were some of the blessings Leo gleaned during our year in Portland at Bible Temple. It was a much needed teaching in the Japanese churches. The Omuta pastor, along with many others, appreciated these biblical truths Leo was sharing.

When we returned to Omuta in 1974, we continued our homeschooling. Steven and Nathan were in their high school studies and Joyce was in the seventh grade. Our children fit right in with the group of sincere young people in the church.

Steven and Nathan, along with others, became leaders in the church's high school youth group. The dedication in the hearts of these young men inspired others in the group to also give themselves wholeheartedly to God. This was a spiritually fulfilling time for our children.

A Very Fulfilling Ministry

Leo set up a Bible school training program in the Omuta church as the pastor had requested him to do. With a love for teaching God's Word, Leo diligently gave himself to it.

All the materials Leo used had to be translated into Japanese, which was a huge challenge. Sato Sensei, a very competent man on the staff of the church, was a great help to Leo in the translation work. It was a tedious, time-consuming job. It took teamwork and patience and hours and hours to accomplish their task. Leo deeply appreciated Sato Sensei's gracious spirit in spite of the time pressures they were working under.

Section by section the material was translated, and section by section Leo taught it to the students. This systematic presentation of God's Word was gratifying. The material they translated into Japanese is still invaluable to this day.

One problem for the Bible school students was how they would support themselves during their time in training. In our area during those days, there were very few part-time jobs available. Some of the young men of the Bible school managed to secure work in Omuta's coal mines. They worked in the mines three days a week--Mondays, Wednesdays, and Fridays. The Bible school classes were held on Tuesdays, Thursdays and Saturdays. The plan worked very well.

Leo was able to fulfill the burden and vision he had carried for many years. It was a time of teaching the Word to *"faithful men who would be able to teach others also" (II Timothy 2:2).*

We wondered what the future held for these young leaders. How would they be used of God in the days ahead? Time would tell.

Pride Rises in the Pastor's Heart

As more years passed, we noticed a change taking place in the heart of the pastor. The success of his ministry had become a source of pride. He desired faster numerical growth in the church and contrived his own ideas and methods to attain it. Instead of ministering spiritual blessings to the people, his main interest became numerical growth. He began carelessly stepping away from biblical principles, principles upon which the church had been established.

This was very distressing to us. Leo cautioned the pastor about diverting from the Word of God. But caution went unheeded.

Occasionally, the pastor would recognize the folly of the direction he was leading the church. He seemingly would have a change of heart and briefly return to biblical principles. But pride and restlessness were still in his spirit. It wasn't long before he would be driving the church again with his own ideas and methods. Diverting away from God's Word and then back again was repeated over and over. It was a source of great frustration for us. We were very concerned for the church.

The Bible school training program also became a target of the pastor's restless ways. Without much warning he would abruptly stop the program saying it was a waste of time. Later, realizing its great value, he would ask Leo to start up the training program again.

Pride was transforming the pastor into a driven man. His unreasonable demands on those under him became increasingly harsh and heavy. Sharp ridicule, often publicly, was inflicted upon many of the leaders and believers. Sometimes he even resorted to physical abuse.

Leo and others repeatedly cautioned the pastor about the way he was abusing the church and the need of pastoring the church in love. His restless, driven spirit refused to take heed.

The pastor began studying the writings and workings of a very influential, radical Buddhist sect. He wanted to learn how they had attracted large numbers into their ranks. The things he read and studied became material for his messages. He used this to chide the people for not working harder to bring more people into the church, venting his anger in the Sunday morning messages.

After exercising much patience in this distressing situation and hoping for a change in the pastor's heart, Leo confronted him again. This time it was not just a caution. Leo clearly told him we could no longer work with him unless he returned to biblical principles for the church. His answer was, "Americans are too concerned about being biblical."

A Very Dark Tunnel

We had been back working in the Omuta church for over twelve years. But now, because of the direction the pastor was forcing upon the church, we felt we could no longer continue working with him.

During those very distressful times the Omuta church was going through, Leo made a number of phone calls to the pastors of our home church in the U.S. Leo explained to these men, in whom we had much confidence, about our situation. We were in a very dark tunnel and we needed their wisdom and counsel.

We also greatly respected my father's counsel. Daddy had visited us in Japan on a number of occasions. At one time he lived with us for a whole year. Daddy knew the Omuta church well, and he loved and respected the dedicated believers. At our time of crisis, we phoned Daddy in Washington State telling him the details of what we were going through.

We even contemplated selling our house and returning to the U.S. for a period of time to rethink how we would be able to continue on with our missionary calling. We phoned Daddy again and told him what we were thinking. A few days later, very deeply grieved in his spirit, Daddy called us back. "You can't leave the hurting people. You must do something for them," he counseled us.

Many faithful, steadfast believers in the Omuta church were as distressed as we were. Some of them came to us and said, "That is fine for you to return to America, Sensei. But what are we going to do? We can't continue on in the Omuta church if you aren't there. You have been our buffer in these distressing times. If you leave the church, we are leaving, too. But we have no place to go."

The pastors in our home church in the U.S., in whom we had confided, gave us the same counsel. We should provide a new "sheepfold" for those sheep who were crying for help from this very distressful situation. We accepted this counsel as God's guidance. We committed our steps of doing so into God's gracious Hand.

Later we tell of how God graciously led us.

Our Children Move on in Life

College and Marriage

Rob graduated from Portland Bible College in 1977, and that fall he married his college sweetheart, a classmate. He chose the finest of young ladies. Susan Martin grew up in a missionary home that ministered to the Hispanics along the Texas-Mexico border.

Rob's desire was to return to Japan as a missionary, and Susan, already with a missionary's heart, was happy to join him in that dedication.

Steven and Nathan graduated from high school the spring of 1977. By diligent study Nathan finished the high school requirements a year early. Together the boys entered Portland Bible College that fall.

Steven and Nathan graduated from Portland Bible College in 1981 with honors. The following month, June, Steven married Shelley Dahl, the young lady who had stolen his heart. She was also a student at Portland Bible College. Shelley, with her very cheerful, adventurous spirit was happy to join in Steven's plans to return to Japan as a missionary. This was settled before Steven proposed!

Joyce, after finishing her high school studies in 1980, went to the island of Yakushima to work for a year in the Christian kindergarten there. Takeshita Sensei and his wife, who are very dear friends of our family, are directors of the kindergarten. They took Joyce into their home for that year. Living on the island and helping in the kindergarten was an interesting experience and proved to be a profitable year for Joyce. The fall of the following year, 1981, she entered Portland Bible College, and graduated in 1985, earning her four-year diploma with honors, as did her brothers.

Kaylor family together for Joyce's graduation from Portland Bible College, 1985
(Joel, Joyce, Steven, Melodee, Rob, Nathan)

In May 1983 wedding bells were ringing again. This time it was for Nathan and the godly young lady he had chosen to be his bride, Cindy Puckett. Cindy attended the church in Eugene, Oregon, where Nathan was a member of the pioneering team. In a very beautiful ceremony, Nathan and Cindy's hearts were joined together as man and wife.

Joyce was a young lady of high Christian principles, and she chose a young man of the same principles. Gary Robinson was that young man who fulfilled all of her dreams. Joyce and Gary were married in January 1989. It was with glowing hearts that Leo and I gave Joyce in marriage to such a fine, young man.

Joel enrolled in Portland Bible College in the fall of 1990, and Melodee the following year. After four years of diligent study, Joel graduated in the spring of 1994.

At his graduation he was presented with the award of honor as the outstanding student of the college for that year. Leo and I were glowing in this great honor given to Joel when, completely unexpected, a special award was given to us.

Pastor Dick Iverson, the founder and president of the college, called Leo and me to the platform. He presented us with a plaque in recognition of the outstanding performance each of our children had achieved in college. It was also specified the plaque was in honor of the twenty-five years of homeschooling we had done on the mission field.

What a treasure Leo and I received that day. Our children made dad and mom look exceedingly great, as they have often done.

The date on the plaque is May 15, 1994. To others that is just a date. To me it has special significance. May 15 (1952) was the day I left Seattle on that very first voyage to Japan.

Melodee's diligence in Portland Bible College was a continuation of her diligence in homeschooling. In the process of time, a fel

The award of honor presented to us the day of Joel's graduation from Portland Bible College, May 15, 1994

low class mate became attracted to her and began wooing her heart. Steve Barnhart, the aggressive wooer, grew up in a godly family in northern Idaho. Steve won our hearts, as he did Melodee's.

After receiving her two-year certificate in college, Melodee and Steve were married in May 1994, at Bible Temple. Two large families with strong Christian backgrounds, the Barnharts and the Kaylors, rejoiced in this glorious occasion. Steve took his new bride to the beautiful mountainous country of northern Idaho to live with him happily ever after.

Melodee amazed everyone at her ability to quickly adapt to the lifestyle of the mountains, so different from her growing up in Japan. She now considered everything Steve was involved in as her calling—all the cows, horses, fields, and hay—as well as the home Bible Study he directs. They are members of an excellent church in a nearby community.

As time passed Joel shared with us he had a growing interest in a beautiful young lady who was still a student at Portland Bible College. Kelly McClenahan was blessed with many talents, but her dedication to God and a desire to be a missionary in Japan were some of the things that captured Joel's heart first of all. Joel was planning to return to Japan as a missionary in God's timing, and Kelly embraced this calling with him.

Joel and Kelly were married in December 1996, in a heart-stirring wedding ceremony. When Kelly came down the center aisle, Joel stepped out to meet her. Together they stood there as everyone was led into a wonderful time of worship. Tears found their way down Joel's cheeks. The mother of the groom was seated close by and produced the tissue he needed. Joel and Kelly's love for God, that matched their love for each other, filled the beautiful wedding ceremony.

When you have six wonderful children, you are destined to have six wonderful sons-and-daughters-in-law. Leo and I do. We are blessed!

As each of our children stepped out of the home nest, Leo and I kept our thoughts centered upon the plan God had for their lives. In this way the empty place they left at home was not hounding us. We were able to rejoice as each of them stepped into a great future with God walking by their side.

Missionaries Themselves

Rob and Susan came to Japan as missionaries in 1979. After a few years, they returned to the U.S. for a time. In December 1989, they came to Japan again to resume their missionary calling. By now they had three young children. This time Rob and Susan came to work alongside us in Ariake Bible Church.

Steven and Shelley, with their two little girls, came out to Japan in January 1989 to fulfill their own calling as missionaries. They, too, worked with us in Ariake Bible Church for a time before spreading their wings to pioneer their own church in the Tokyo area. While they were here in Kyushu, another little girl was added to their family. Over the following years, Steven and Shelley received three beautiful Japanese children into their home. We are proud to consider them among our grandchildren.

Steven wrote an excellent book in Japanese, *The Healthy Church*. It was an outgrowth of a series of messages he ministered on the subject in many churches across Japan. It was published in 2003 and has been a great inspiration to pastors and churches.

Joel and Kelly, with their two children, began their missionary career in Japan the summer of 2007. After working with Steven and Shelley in Tokyo for a year or so, they plan to pioneer their own ministry.

1987 and Onward

Significant Milestones

Ariake Bible Church

In October 1987 we determined we had no other choice but to step out of the Omuta church. We stated our final decision to the pastor that we could no longer work with him because of the unscriptural direction in which he was persistently going. He clearly let us know he had no intentions of changing that direction.

On a Sunday morning a couple of weeks later, we gathered with a group of believers in a community hall in Arao, a neighboring city of Omuta. It was a group of believers who had experienced much distress in the past few years because of the direction the Omuta church was being driven. It had been a long, dark tunnel for all of us. That Sunday morning was the first service of the new "sheepfold." We offered sacrifices of praise that day.

Ariake Bible Church was the name the believers chose for the newly formed church. Ariake is the name of a large bay near us, and much of the area around us is known as Ariake Region.

We came up with our own meaning for the two characters for "Ari-ake". "Ari" is the word used in the Bible for "I AM," and "ake" can mean, "breaking forth of the dawn." Therefore, to us, the word "Ariake" has come to mean "The brilliant breaking forth of the great I AM."

Church Land

As a newly organized church, Ariake Bible Church had no facilities of its own. Using community halls for our weekly meetings provided places for us to hold our church services. No place would allow us to use their facilities on a continued weekly basis. For our Sunday worship services, we were compelled to alternate between community halls.

There were a few times when a meeting place could not be secured. On those occasions we set up our equipment in a designated park and the believers gathered there for Sunday morning worship. Such times deepened the people's desire for a permanent location of their own. The plan was to buy land and build our own church facilities. We calculated we would need about a half an acre of land for the building and parking lot. Finding a piece of land that size was more difficult than we had anticipated. The church members searched diligently far and near for a permanent location for our church.

Leo went to a land realtor on several occasions and asked if there were any such pieces of land available. Each time the realtor replied, "Sensei, it will be very difficult to find a piece of land the size you say you want. There just isn't anything like that available. If I do hear of something, I will call you."

Months went by and Leo made the trek again to the realtor's office. Again he was told, "Sensei, there is no land of that size available."

As a church we continued praying and searching for the right piece of land, all the while adding to our land fund in the bank. The fund was growing little by little. By now we had been using rented facilities for our church services for about three years.

Time was going by and no progress was being made to find what we desired in a piece of land. Going back to the realtor's office again and again became more difficult each time for Leo.

The answer was always the same, "No land of that size is available. I'll call you if I find something."

More months went by. I nudged Leo, "Dear, why don't you try going to the realtor one more time." Faith welled up in Leo's spirit. With freshness in his determination, he again set out for the realtor's office. But the response was the same, "There just isn't anything available, Sensei."

However, that day as Leo sat there talking, the realtor's phone rang. After a short conversation, he put down the receiver, and turning to Leo and said excitedly, *"Sensei, tochi ga arimasu yo!!"* ("Sensei, there *is* a piece of land!").

He then explained the phone call was from a realtor friend of his. A large piece of land had just become available the day before. The realtor described the location to Leo and he knew exactly where it was--only about two miles from our house.

Jubilantly Leo came home and told me. We looked at it together—a beautiful piece of land, excellently located on a well-traveled road on the outskirts of Arao City. When the leaders of the church saw the land, they were all in agreement that this was the half-acre of land for which we had been praying and searching. We knew God had provided this land for us. Over a period of months, the bank loan which we needed was approved, and the deal was finalized. On October 15, 1991, the land became the property of Ariake Bible Church.

Unearthed Bones

Part of the land the church had purchased was a rice paddy, and the rest was a garden plot. The land was on two levels and needed some work done to make it suitable for the church building and the parking lot. There was also a small bamboo thicket at the back corner of the property.

We contracted the work that needed to be done on the land. Soon bulldozers and other land-moving equipment were hard at work. This was progress that was exciting to watch.

The job hadn't progressed far when one day the foreman frantically phoned Leo. He was greatly distressed. "Sensei, the workers came upon some human bones under the bamboo thicket at the corner of the property. All the workers have fled and won't return to work until you come and pray for the peace of the dead who have been so rudely disturbed!"

A veterinarian was called and the bones were confirmed to be human. (Incidentally, when the veterinarian saw Leo, his memory went back thirty years. He remarked he had been a student in the fifth grade classroom when Leo sat at the back of the room to audit the class.)

Since the bones were confirmed to be human, it was a serious matter. We contacted the police. After studying the situation, the police concluded the bones could possibly be the remains of soldiers from Japan's Southwest Civil War of 1877. That war had been fought in this area of Kyushu. Soldiers had probably been killed and quickly buried, and then bamboo planted there to conceal the burial place.

The police determined it was a very old, unmarked grave; therefore no further research needed to be done. We were instructed to just gather all the bones into large, plastic baskets like those used in vegetable gardens. The police would then come to dispose of the bones.

If it had been an official, marked grave, it would have presented a very grave problem indeed! Months and months of research would have been involved. We could not have continued with our land preparations until the time consuming research had been done. Marked graves, no matter how old, are not carelessly disturbed.

The following Sunday afternoon, which happened to be Easter, we planned a time of worship and prayer at our land site to pacify the foreman and his workers. A group of believers gathered for the service. Easter flowers from our morning worship service were placed nearby. The singing of hymns and rejoicing on this Easter Sunday afternoon made an impression on the foreman and the workers. They stood silently by with heads bowed. Leo prayed a prayer of thanksgiving to God for all He had done for us. No mention was made of the occupants of the grave.

With that done the men gladly returned the following day to continue their work. They sifted through the dirt and collected all the bones. It turned out to be the remains of five or six individuals in the hidden grave. No one knew the true details, only that the grave was determined to be very old. The police had come to their conclusions. With that they were satisfied. However, we wondered about another possibility concerning the grave.

Kyushu had been the place of intense persecution and martyrdom of Christians for 250 years, up to as late as 1850. Thousands of devout believers stood true to their faith and became martyrs. Could it be that Christian martyrs were in that unmarked, hidden grave? Could it be that God had destined a church to be built on that land in honor of those faithful Christians? We have wondered.

Drawing Floor Plans

Now that Ariake Bible Church had purchased land, we were focusing on progress toward the church building. It would be a while before we could actually get into that big project. All monies, for now, were going toward paying off the land.

A detailed floor plan for the church building became a primary need. From high school days, I had enjoyed drawing floor plans. Now with this big challenge before me, I was anxious to see what kind of a floor plan I could come up with. I mused at why God had put within me an enjoyment of drawing floor plans. Was it for such a time as this?

Many evenings I would get out my drawing material—graph paper, pencil, eraser and ruler—and progress a bit further on the plans. To me it was exciting; I enjoyed it. I ended up spending hours and hours working on the drawings. Hours stretched into days, days into weeks, and weeks into months. Eventually the months turned into two years that I was continually measuring, changing, and improving the plans.

Leo and I still laugh about the places we measured to help in the details of making the drawings. One day we came upon a stairwell of a certain restaurant that seemed perfect in size for a stairwell we were planning in the church building. My measuring tape was always close at hand. Since no one was around, we quickly measured the width of that stairwell and the depth of its steps. Those measurements became fixed in the floor plans. At other times I measured such things as toilet stalls. We wanted every detail of the church to be as user-friendly as possible. The floor plans eventually evolved into a product with which we were pleased.

We made a trip to the U.S. in 1993 for a short stay. We took the detailed, but simple, unprofessional floor plans with us. In the U.S. a retired architect, Mel Walters, a kindly Christian man, offered to translate the drawings into official blueprints.

Mel painstakingly translated those few pages of graph paper drawings into pages and pages of blueprints. A very minimal price was all he asked for his excellent work. Now we had the needed blueprints in our hands. This was progress toward our church building.

We were saddened to learn later that Mel passed away before our building became a reality. His kindnesses are imprinted on our hearts and on our building.

Church Structure

The believers of Ariake Bible Church, with their sacrificial gifts and offerings, were financing the entire project of the church land and building. The half-acre of land we purchased had cost $500,000. We estimated the cost of the building would be similar.

Leo, our son Rob (Rob, Susan and their family had returned to Japan in 1989 to minister with us in the church), and others had done much research to determine what type of construction we should use for the church. Japan primarily used concrete and steel for their building structures, but that was very expensive. However, some churches in Japan were now constructing their new buildings using imported materials from the U.S. It was considerably cheaper than the concrete and steel structures.

During one of our trips to the U.S., we looked into the possibility of using American materials for our church. We discussed the situation with a good friend of the family, Steve Dahl. He had been a close friend of Steven and Nathan since their days together in Portland Bible college. Steven had married Steve Dahl's younger sister, Shelley.

Steve owned and operated his own construction company. When he heard our story, he told Leo, "Once a year I give a portion of my time to go to a foreign country to construct buildings for the Kingdom of God. I will go out to Japan with a team of carpenters and build your church for you. Just supply food and lodging for the carpenters and we will donate our labor." We were overwhelmed. We accepted Steve's most gracious offer with much thanksgiving.

With that decision made, we needed to order all the building materials in the U.S. and have them shipped in containers to Japan via ocean freighters. We needed professional help for the ordering and assembling of these materials.

Once again we benefited from a family connection. Rod Robinson, an older brother of our daughter Joyce's husband, Gary, offered to order all the building materials at wholesale cost through his private construction company in Vancouver, Washington. Step by step we were walking through wide open doors made possible by dedicated servants of God.

Rod Robinson set to work on our project. Three large containers were filled with framing materials for the first phase of the building. Those containers were shipped in mid-January 1995 from Seattle via Pusan, South Korea. They would be routed from Pusan to a Kyushu port near us. The containers would then be trucked to our building site, arriving around the first part of February.

Steve Dahl and a team of four other carpenters had volunteered to give three weeks of their very valuable time for the first phase of our church building project. They were prepared to fly out from the U.S. and arrive at our land site the same time the containers would arrive. It was a good plan.

Then suddenly—!

We were not prepared for what happened next!

A Devastating Earthquake

A devastating earthquake struck the port city of Kobe, Japan, on January 17, 1995. The damage and death toll of the quake was astronomical. At the time of the earthquake, the containers filled with our building materials were somewhere on the high seas.

Kobe Port, which handles thousands of containers from all over the world, was totally destroyed. Consequently, all the incoming containers that were headed for Kobe were suddenly re-routed to Pusan. Our three containers ended up in that massive confusion of containers that piled up in Pusan Port.

An official at our local port did his best in his contacts with Pusan to locate our containers, but with little success. We were told it might be three to six weeks before our containers could be dislodged from the logjam at the Korean port. We needed God to help us and we prayed earnestly for His intervention.

By now, according to plan, the five carpenters had already arrived in Tokyo. The men were to spend a few days sightseeing before flying down to Kyushu. They had purchased their return tickets to the U.S. in accordance with the three weeks they had allotted themselves to complete the first phase of our building. Every day counted. However, the containers with our building materials were nowhere in sight.

Those were tense days. Then, by the persistence of the local port official, things started happening. Our three containers were finally located in Pusan, shipped to Kyushu and trucked to our building site. The team of five carpenters had arrived in Kyushu and were standing with us the morning those three big trucks with the containers rolled onto the church land. That was a moment of great rejoicing. The building project was started immediately. Hardly a day of the scheduled work plan had been lost.

Building Project

Our church building project took eight months from beginning to completion—February to October 1995. During those months, a total of eighteen carpenters, many of them professionals, came from the U.S. to donate their expertise and time. Each of them spent two to three weeks with us laboring diligently on our building. We remain greatly indebted to all of them.

A Kaylor team of carpenters' helpers worked side-by-side with the professional men throughout the building project. The Kaylor team consisted of Leo, Rob, Joel, and Rob's son David.

Joel had graduated from Bible college. He gave a year to come and help in our building project. He had a dedication in his heart to return to Japan as a missionary in God's time. David was now a bean pole of fifteen years. His ear-to-ear perpetual smile could almost appear to out-measure his waist. He lacked nothing in his amazing ability to work side by side with the carpenters.

The men of our church joined in the work force as often as their time would allow them. The ladies, in groups of three or four, supplied excellent meals for all the workers.

During the months when no professional carpenters were here, Rob acted as foreman for many things that could be accomplished by the Kaylor team and the men of the church. Thus, nail upon nail, board upon board, day upon day, progress was being made on the building.

The final team of five carpenters came in October to finish all that was yet to be done. Steve Dahl came again with that team. Steve had supervised the beginning of the building in February, and he wanted to supervise the finishing, as well. And so it was. Our beautiful church building was completed in October 1995.

Church Dedication

In the eighth year after Ariake Bible Church was formed, we moved into our new church building. God had faithfully guided us through all the blessings, and He had walked beside us when struggles came.

The Ariake Bible Church congregation had sacrificed with liberal offerings for the land and church building. Now they were rejoicing in the fruit of their sacrifices.

That fall in November 1995, we planned a three-day conference which would include the dedication of our new facilities. It was a special blessing for Leo and me to have all four of our sons here for that time of great rejoicing.

Ariake Bible Church completed October 1995

Steven and his family came from Tokyo, and Nathan brought his family all the way from Eugene, Oregon. Rob and his family were already here, of course, and Joel was still with us after almost a year of helping with the construction of the church building.

It was decided that we would have our son Steven as the guest speaker for the fall conference and dedication service. Steven and Shelley had spent the first two years of their missionary career ministering in Ariake Bible Church. They had now been in pioneer work in Tokyo for four years. They were greatly loved by our congregation.

Pastors and believers from all over Kyushu and from other places further away came to celebrate with Ariake Bible Church for this special occasion. Almighty God had blessed us, and we were giving Him honor with our praises.

Rob Becomes Senior Pastor in 1999

Ariake Bible Church was moving on in blessings. Rob and Susan had been working with us in the church for about ten years. Rob's giftings of pastoring were well proven. The leadership of the church agreed it was time to pass the torch of senior pastor to Rob.

There were men in the congregation who were wholly dedicated to God and His purposes for the church. They conducted their lives upon the Word of God. A group of these men with their wives would also be set in as elders and deacons of Ariake Bible Church.

The setting in of Rob and Susan as senior pastors, and the elders and deacons as leaders in the church, would be on Sunday afternoon, June 13. It would be the highlight of a three-day conference.

We had invited Pastor Mike Herron from Salem, Oregon, to be the special speaker for the conference. He is a highly respected man of God, well known for his great gift of music and prophetic mantle. Pastor Mike had already blessed Ariake Bible Church with his anointed ministry on several previous occasions.

Steven, along with his family, came from Tokyo to share in the conference. Joel and his family and Rob's son, David, who was now enrolled in Portland Bible College, came from Portland. Pastors and their believers from around Kyushu gathered to rejoice with us.

On that memorable Sunday afternoon, June 13, Leo waxed eloquent in the remarks he made. He had everyone listening intently as he intertwined Kaylor family history and the history of Ariake Bible Church. Included in Leo's remarks, he made reference to the old German Bible that had been purchased by the Kohler family (spelling later changed to Kaylor) in 1790 in a German settlement on America's east coast. This old family treasure had been passed from generation to generation for two hundred years. Leo's father had presented it to him in 1961.

Rob became senior pastor of Ariake Bible Church June 13, 1999.

Only Leo and I knew what was in the package he had taken with him to the platform. At the appropriate moment, Leo asked Rob to join him on the platform. Leo took the old German Bible from the package. Moved with emotions he said, "Rob, today I present this old family treasure to you." It was a sacred moment. There was hardly a dry eye present. Father and son embraced. Rob represented the eighth generation to receive the treasured German Bible.

The service moved on with great rejoicing. Rob and Susan were prayed and prophesied over and proclaimed as senior pastors of Ariake Bible Church. Then the elders and deacons, with their wives, were set in with prayer and proclamations. No one was as happy as Leo and I.

Celebrating Fifty Years in Japan (2002)

As the story has been written, Leo came to Japan in December 1951. I came May 1952. We were married May 1953.

As the fifty-year milestone of our ministry in Japan was approaching, Ariake Bible Church leaders began thinking of plans for celebrating. They wanted to express their appreciation for our years of ministry in the best way possible.

The date for the three-day celebration was set for July 26-28, 2002. Ariake Bible Church decided to pay the fare for all of our children to come to Japan for the celebrations. Nothing could have pleased Leo and me more. All the children had played an important part in our ministry.

At the appointed time in July, our children arrived at the Fukuoka airport along with some of the spouses and some of the grandchildren. We met them as they came off the plane. What a jolly good time we had hugging little necks and big necks and then hugging them all over again.

Our fun-loving family at the celebration of our fifty years of ministry in Japan
(Joel, Joyce, Steven, Rob, Melodee, Nathan)

Kaylor family members who were able to come for the celebration totaled twenty-five. We arranged for families to be comfortably situated in a nearby hotel. Others lodged in our home and in Rob's.

It was in the plans that Rob, Steven, and Joel would be the speakers for the conference. Nathan, Joyce, and Melodee also shared their hearts with the people. Leo and I were bursting with thanksgiving and pride as each of the six either preached or shared. A number of the older people in the congregation had watched our children grow up from ordinary children into the men and women of God they now are. Some of the young parents who attended the conference spoke to us of the encouragement our children's testimonies were to them. It gave them hope for their own children!

Sunday afternoon, the 28th, was the grand finale. Leo and I were highly honored by all of our children, by our church, and by many pastors and friends who came to also express their appreciation for our fifty years of ministry in Japan. We felt abundantly rewarded for all we had walked through in those fifty years.

We were honored by a group of tambourine dancers.

Our Fiftieth Wedding Anniversary (2003)

Our children asked us what our wishes were for celebrating our fiftieth wedding anniversary. More than anything else, Leo and I preferred it to be just a family time together.

No place would be more appropriate for our fun-loving family to gather for the occasion than at Steve and Melodee's home in the mountains of northern Idaho. The date was set for May 23-26, 2003. Leo and I, Rob and Susan, and Steven and Shelley would fly from Japan to the U.S. to join the rest of the family for this special occasion.

Steve and Melodee's big hearts were wide open to host the family gathering at their home. Their log home is spacious. But how can thirty-one family members possibly squeeze in?

Steve's parents, Phillip and Patsy Barnhart, live only a short way down the hill from Steve and Melodee. When they heard of

Celebrating fifty wonderful years together

the Kaylor family gathering for our fiftieth wedding anniversary, they graciously offered their wonderful home to be used to house some of us.

Phillip and Patsy had recently built a beautiful new addition onto their house. Their purpose in this new addition of rooms was to provide a place where missionaries, pastors, or others could come who needed a place to rest and rejuvenate. Such are the hospitality-filled hearts of Phillip and Patsy Barnhart.

Posing with our six children and their spouses.
Back: Susan and Rob Kaylor, Cindy and Nathan Kaylor,
*   Kelly and Joel Kaylor, Shelley and Steven Kaylor,*
*   Melodee and Steve Barnhart.*
Front: Gary and Joyce Robinson.

The Family Gathered

Friday, May 23 arrived. It was the appointed day for the family to gather in the beautiful Idaho mountains. By late afternoon carload by carload of excited travelers rumbled up the last leg of the long journey. The end of the road, literally, was their destination—Steve and Melodee's wonderful home that was ready to welcome us.

All the cars seemed to be arriving at the same time. Everyone had hugs and kisses for everyone. Then another car came chugging up the hill. It was a single occupant I didn't seem to recognize.

I looked again. Stepping out of the bright red, little car was Carolyn Evans, Leo's niece (a daughter of Leo's sister Eilene) who came all the way from Ohio. She flew to Spokane, Washington, and then drove the final way in a rented car. What a grand surprise Carolyn added to our happy family. Apparently it was a surprise to only Leo and me. Our children already knew about Carolyn's coming but kept it a secret from us.

Leo's brother Roy, with his wife Louise, joined our family in Idaho for the celebrations.

Leo's brother Roy, with his wife Louise, also made the journey all the way from Houston, Texas. They were very special guests of honor. Over the past fifty years we had only limited times of being together. It was indeed an honor to have Roy and Louise join us.

The following morning, Saturday the 24th, the house was abuzz from an early hour. Horseback riding was a favorite that lured the younger ones out of bed. Breakfast was self-service; everyone had brought food to share. The house was bulging with the jubilant crowd—the talking, the laughing, and the sharing never ceased.

The Celebrations

The children had planned the special celebrations for Saturday evening. Leo and I were escorted to the nearby community hall at 4:00 p.m. The rest of the family were already there. What a radiant family we were, all dressed in our finest.

Joyce pinned beautiful corsages on Leo and me. Mine was a large white orchid—chosen because I had carried an orchid on a white Bible on our wedding day fifty years ago.

My sister Zella and her husband Herb, along with their daughter and granddaghter, had driven four hours just to spend the evening of celebration with us. How special to have them come.

A buffet of food, second to no place in the whole world, so we said, was spread out. Steve's mother Patsy with her sister Trudy excelled in their giftings in preparing this banquet for us.

Joel, so impressive in a tuxedo, was the emcee that evening. We worshipped and sang. Thanksgiving poured out of our hearts to our great God for all He had done for us. The evening was filled with much laughter and many joyful tears. Leo and I were blessed with the very finest of celebrations. All the great things the children did and said and the love that flowed among us was an exceedingly great treasure.

Another Day of Blessings Together

Sunday was another day of blessing together. It dawned early for some of us—and later for others. Steve's huckleberry pancakes started the day out. Again the eating process moved along smoothly. It wasn't *"the early bird gets the worm,"* as there was plenty for everyone, early risers and the later ones.

We were all looking forward to our Sunday morning worship together. At the appointed time, the living room was packed with worshipers. It was even more glorious than we had anticipated. No worship leader, no message, no offering. Just worshiping and sharing together. It was a precious time lingering in God's Presence.

Little cousins, after a full day of play, dropped off to sleep one by one while watching a video.

In the afternoon some of us piled into Steve's pickup for a ride up the mountain road—a road that, part of the time, only Steve knew was there. After a distance of bumping and bouncing along, a closed gate indicated that was as far as the pickup could go. We then hiked on up the mountain ridge where we had a panoramic view of Pend Oreille Lake (pronounced Pond O-ray) and on beyond into Montana.

That evening, after a supper of curry rice, we gathered in the living room again for another time of worship. Our hearts were overflowing.

Monday morning was the time for the return trip back down the mountain. One by one, family cars pulled away. Everyone mustered smiles and cheerful good-byes. It had been a marvelous three days together. Precious memories live on.

The Kaylor family at our "fiftieth" celebrations.
Five grandchildren (in Japan) not in picture.

Planting Churches

Young Men Pioneer Churches *(by Leo)*

Several of the young men who had been in the Omuta Bible training program (1975-1985) had married. They were anticipating pioneering their own churches.

As those young pastors started out in the ministry, they valued biblical principles, and the importance of the local church.

Kunio Nishida Sensei and his wife, Ritsuko, moved to Fukuoka and began pioneering a church in that city in 1990. A number of young people from the Omuta church teamed up with Nishida Sensei in the church plant of Fukuoka Harvest Church.

In 1992 they purchased land and built their own church facilities. The church congregation continues to grow in number, and the building is now filled to capacity with two worship services on Sunday mornings.

Nishida Sensei caught the vision of training leaders in the local church. From the beginning of their church plant in Fukuoka, he started a training program for his emerging young leaders. He asked my assistance in occasionally teaching some of the Bible courses.

Nishida Sensei has continued his training program, and through the years succeeding groups of young people have been preparing for the ministry.

Yoji Nakamura San was one of the young men in the first group of trainees. He and his wife became the youth leaders for the high school group in Fukuoka Harvest Church, where they ministered effectively for six years.

In 2002 Nakamura Sensei and his wife were sent out to pioneer a new church in Kumamoto. That church is now a healthy, growing nucleus of believers. After meeting in rented facilities for several years, they are now earnestly looking for land to buy. They hope to soon build permanent facilities of their own.

The Spirit of God has brought about a network of a number of Kyushu churches flowing in harmony. We are blessed to be a part of this fellowship.

The following are moving stories of how God worked in the lives of Nishida Sensei and of Nakamura Sensei to bring them to His salvation.

My Testimony of How I Met Jesus

by Kunio Nishida
Senior Pastor of Fukuoka Harvest Church
Written in 2006
(Translated by Leo Kaylor)

One Sunday evening late in the fall as I was walking along the shopping district of downtown Omuta, a smiling, young lady approached me. She was a Christian and she handed me an invitation to attend a gospel meeting that evening. It was the first time for me to have any contact with Christianity.

That was thirty-two years ago and I was twenty-five years old at the time. I had no interest in Christianity. However, I did have plenty of free time, and because the Christians were so zealous, I began attending the gospel meetings in the public hall each Sunday night.

One of the men at the meeting hall often talked to me about the Bible. At one time he invited me to his home for a meal. As we ate I sensed the warm and friendly atmosphere of their home—it seemed so comfortable. By just being in the fellowship of their

Nishida Sensei

home, I experienced a very wonderful healing in my heart. The husband treated his wife with great respect; the children responded freely to the kindness of their parents. In a sense of shock, I thought to myself, "Is it really possible that if you become a Christian you can have a home like this?"

That Christian home was such a contrast to my home where I grew up. My father was very short-tempered and was always yelling at us. My mother worked like a slave. We were very poor and, as children, we each had to work hard. But seeing how my father mistreated my mother was the most painful of all.

The image I had of Christians was totally changed, and I made a decision to seriously seek to become a Christian. However, after about three months, I lost interest. I began to think, "It's no use for me to try to become a Christian. I don't want to give up my drinking, smoking, gambling, and amusements. This has been a good, little experiment for me, but I will quit going to their meetings." With that decision my mind became lighter and I felt relieved.

However, the very next morning while riding the train to work, I began thinking, "Where does a person go when he dies?" The Christians had said, according to the Bible, sinners go to hell. "What is hell like?" They had told me "Hell is the lake of fire!" I became troubled in my mind again. I worked at the fire station and I knew how terrible fire can be.

I decided to go back to the gospel meeting one more time. I asked myself, "Is God really alive?" The Christians had said, "God is alive." If God is really alive, I want to meet Him.

I took a week off from work and started out on a trip with no pre-determined destination. I found a cheap hotel and began to read the Bible and other gospel books I had brought along.

The first day and the second day passed and I thought, "It's about time to meet Jesus!" But nothing happened. The Bible says to fast, so I fasted for two days. Still nothing happened. I had taken off work for a whole week, spent all that money, and sincerely sought after God. I was getting discouraged.

The next day was Sunday and I decided to go to church one last time. If I felt nothing, I would stop going to church for good. The church service proceeded as usual with nothing special happening in my heart. At the close of the service, the pastor said, "Everyone please stand and we will sing hymn number 300." The song was, "Onward Christian Soldiers." As we began to sing, suddenly I felt my heart being touched with something warm. I heard a Voice saying, "I love you and you are My soldier!" At the same time, I felt the love of God cover me like a great wave. It was like I was being embraced by a warm personality. I had never before in my life felt anything like this.

I had been touched by the love of God. I was so happy I just wept and couldn't stop the tears. I cried out in my heart, "Oh yes, God is Love. God loves me! God, the Creator of heaven and earth knows someone like me." This experience was beyond anything I could imagine.

My life was completely transformed by this experience. I was so filled with joy that I began to tell everyone about Jesus. When I was driving my car, songs of joy spilled from my mouth. When I went to church, I could have fellowship with the other Christians just like they were my family.

I realized I had been totally transformed. I stopped drinking, smoking, and gambling. However, the greatest transformation in my heart was that I could forgive my father.

I began to think, "It is so sad that my father does not know Jesus." My father was now in the hospital with a lung disease, and I had not gone to see him even once. After God touched my life, I visited my father in the hospital, and he was so happy to see me.

My father had fervently worshipped idols all his life, but now he became a Christian. My mother, too, became a Christian. I experienced the joy of serving Jesus. With that joy I entered into training to prepare for the ministry. God gave me a wonderful wife and three children. I, along with my wife, now pastor a happy, family-oriented church in Fukuoka.

From Problem Child to Pastor

By Yoji Nakamura
Pastor of Kumamoto Harvest Church
Written in 2006
(Translated by Leo Kaylor)

I went to church for the first time when I was in the seventh grade. I lived in Fukuoka at that time. Once a month I attended the joint worship service that was held in the central church in Omuta. Even now I cannot forget the scene that met my eyes—the image I had of church was totally changed. The service was full of life, and people's faces were radiant with joy.

Nakamura Sensei

One thing that impressed me was a very gentle missionary and his wife with their big smiles. They were Leo and Phyllis Kaylor whom I came to love and respect.

Before I was saved, I had completely lost all hope for living. My mother had died of cancer when I was in the fifth grade. The construction company which my father managed had acquired huge debts and went bankrupt. About two years after my mother passed away, my father fled one night, leaving us four children to fend for ourselves. My older sister and I had to find part-time work to support the four of us.

It was in the midst of all of these troubles that I first went to church. I met the Lord Jesus Christ as my Savior and from that moment on my life was transformed. I had lost all hope in living, but now God gave me a future and a hope.

After I graduated from high school, I enrolled in Bible school. I studied some Bible courses by correspondence. Also, Kaylor Sensei taught courses at church on the Holy Spirit and on the local church. As students, we all sat on the *tatami* mat floor in a small room, while

Kaylor Sensei stood up by the whiteboard as he taught. Because of his height, I remember we all had sore necks from looking up so far!

Nishida Sensei and his wife are excellent pastors of the church in Fukuoka where I was saved. I experienced many wonderful blessings under their ministry. Nishida Sensei asked me to be the youth leader; I served in that capacity for six years. During that time I married a beautiful, Christian, young lady. God soon blessed our home with two little girls. Ten years later, another baby girl was added to us.

After six years as youth leaders, my wife and I were sent out to pioneer a new church in Kumamoto. I remembered Kaylor Sensei's teaching on the local church. It helped me set up the structure for my own church.

Two years ago I became a prison chaplain in the Kumamoto Penitentiary. Last year three prisoners were saved and baptized.

Our church is a "grandchild" church of Kaylor Sensei's ministry. He started the church in Omuta, and the church in Fukuoka grew out of Omuta. I was trained in the Fukuoka church and was sent out to pioneer in Kumamoto.

Kaylor Sensei's passion for evangelism and for healthy church structure continues to flow into the very formation and pulse of our church in Kumamoto.

Stories of God at Work

Matsue Mitarai *(by Leo)*

Matsue Mitarai began attending our church around 1959. She brought her six year old daughter, Ritsuko, with her. (Ritsuko later became the wife of Nishida Sensei, pastor of Fukuoka Harvest Church.) We look back over more than forty-five years we have known Mitarai San. She and her family have been a blessing to our church and to other churches.

At the time of Mitarai San's ninetieth birthday, she was reminiscing with us about her life. We asked her to write the story of how she was saved and of her walk with the Lord. This story will give you insights into life in Japan in the days before and after World War II.

A Redeemed Life

By Matsue Mitarai
Written 2004
(Translated by Leo Kaylor)

I was born in 1913 into a very poor family in a rural farming area of Kagoshima Prefecture in southern Japan. It was rare for a young person from our village to be accepted into college for school teachers' training. However, my brother received that honor.

It was impossible for my father, with his income as a carpenter, to pay my brother's college expenses. Knowing this, I wanted to help my family in whatever way I could. So I decided to go to Osaka (a large city five hundred miles away) to get a job and help pay my brother's college bill. I was only fifteen years old at that time.

I read many different books at the factory where I worked. I read something that had an impact upon me. It was written by a Christian: "Try throwing a small stone into a calm, still lake. It will make a circular ripple which will continue to expand on and on. In the same way, a person's thoughts and actions, whether good or bad, are like waves that begin to move in a person's heart. They will exceed time and space and continue to expand indefinitely. Therefore, produce good waves from a source of joy!"

When I read this, I became conscious of my sin. I feared I could never get away from the memory of sin for as long as I lived. (An incident that Mitarai San considered dishonest troubled her deeply.) I wanted to find a religion, whatever it might be, that could cancel out and forgive my sin. When I asked about such a religion, one of the older factory workers told me he had heard that Christianity teaches your sins can be forgiven.

I went to town immediately. When I met a person who seemed to be sincere, I would ask, "Can you tell me where there is a Christian church?" Along the way one person answered, "That looks like a church over there." I went to investigate. It was a Holiness Church.

I began attending the services of that church each week. In time I understood that Christ died on the cross to forgive our sins. I determined that, regardless of what might happen, I would never turn away from this God. I was baptized in a cold river in Kobe on December 6, 1931.

I eventually returned to my home town in Kyushu, but there was not one church in all of the surrounding area. I hoped that some day I could live in a place where there was a church. I also determined that, if I were to get married, I would absolutely not marry anyone who either smoked or drank.

One day I received a marriage proposal from a man who worked in the Mitsui Coal Mining Company in Omuta, in the northern part of Kyushu Island. My father and mother said, "The Mitsui Company is a good company in Japan, and this man is a sincere man who does not smoke or drink. What do you think about marrying him?"

In my heart I was thinking there should be a church in the large city of Omuta, and this man doesn't smoke or drink. I answered my parents, "If he would be happy with someone like me, I will go." I had not met the man nor seen his picture, but I made my decision to marry him.

Finally the day of the wedding arrived. I was twenty-one and he was thirty-one. In my country village, it was customary at a wedding reception dinner, which was the beginning of the wedding, for all of the men to sit on one side of the room and the women to sit on the other side. I was dressed as a bride and so was easily recognized in the line of women. All the men wore the same kind of formal suits. I could not tell which one of those men was to be my husband.

After we were married, I moved to Omuta and began my new life. My husband turned out to be a very stern man. I found life had become very rigid and stressed. It was as though at all times, I was sitting face to face with a very stern teacher. We did not have a child for four or five years. I did not tell my husband that I was attending church, nor that I also had subscribed to a Christian magazine.

One time my husband let me return to visit my country home in Kagoshima. While I was away, he found some of my Christian magazines I had hidden in the closet. When I came home, he scolded me severely with a loud, angry voice. "You are studying a terrible religion!" However, I knew in my heart there was nothing bad written in the magazines. His accusations didn't disturb me.

A few days passed and he said, "Don't you ever go to church again!" I obeyed what my husband demanded and did not go to church. Then several months later, he said in his stern way, "Okay. You can go to church." I can remember how happy I was.

Later God blessed us with one, two, and three children. I praised God for them.

Then the Pacific War broke out. It became such a difficult time. We could hardly make ends meet on my husband's meager income. Because of the many bombings during the war, our city of Omuta had become like a burned-off field. It was a horrible sight. The war ended August 15, 1945, and we were set free from the fear of any more bombing attacks.

My husband had been forced by the coal mining company to work far beyond his strength. He was like a rubber band that had been stretched beyond its endurance. Then it snapped under the strain. He contracted a terrible lung disease. At that time he became too weak to even go to the *benjo* without help. I was at my wits end to know what to do.

My husband said to me, "Just consider that I am dead. Go out and find whatever kind of work you can." From then on I was thrown into a frenzied daze trying to keep enough food on our table. I tried a sales job. I was not accustomed to going door-to-door as a salesperson trying to sell things. I was so miserable. I felt like a beggar and was so dejected. I tried all kinds of different jobs, all the while taking my small children with me.

At one time I fasted for three days while continuing with my strenuous work load. I didn't know much about fasting, and I went without food and water for three days. The evening of the third day I lost all my strength and became so terribly dizzy I almost collapsed. However, through all of this, I did not stop going to church. I constantly had a heavy heart; I longed to be able to lead my husband into faith in Christ.

One day my husband suddenly got a very severe headache. He went to the Fukuoka University Hospital and to other good hospitals as well, but the doctors all said, "We cannot find what is causing your headaches." My husband gave up all hope of getting well.

I was always praying for him to be saved. At that time I said to a Christian brother, Oota Sensei, "My husband has a terrible headache. Please come to my house and pray for him." He willingly came and brought a missionary, Bernie Blackstone, with him. Blackstone Sensei did not understand Japanese very well, but he came and prayed earnestly. My husband was deeply touched by his prayer and promised, "I don't understand much, but if my headache goes away, I will certainly go to church."

A short time later, my husband's terrible headache was gone. Just as he had promised, he sincerely began attending church. He was wonderfully saved and was baptized by Leo Kaylor Sensei. Kaylor Sensei and his wife poured love and kindness upon my husband. Years later when my husband was in the hospital, they visited him nearly every week. My husband has now gone to heaven.

My three children are all Christians. My son and his family live in Osaka and faithfully attend church there. One of my daughters, Ritsuko, is the pastor's wife of the Fukuoka Harvest Church. My grandchildren are all serving the Lord.

I feel as though no one is as blessed as I am. I am now ninety years old, but I still love to dig in my big garden and raise vegetables and flowers. I am always telling others about the blessings of God in my life. I carry gospel tracts in my handbag and share the gospel with those I meet. That is my joy. Hallelujah!

At 92, Mitarai San still enjoys working in her garden.

Her husband also became a fervent Christian.

How I Found Christ

By Shigeko Ogura
Written 2005
(Translated by Leo Kaylor)

Shigeko Ogura

When I was a child of three and a half years, I was adopted by foster parents who had no children of their own. It was soon after World War II, and for most people, life was lived with meager supply.

My adoptive father was one of the many workers in the Omuta coal mines. It was very hard work. My adoptive mother was a tidy person. She was skillful with her hands and made clothes for me. When I enrolled in elementary school, my parents actively participated in the school functions. In this way they showed their love for me.

However, when I was about ten years old, home life became very stressed and erratic. My mother began to deal very harshly with me. She made me prepare my own breakfasts; she called it discipline. For some reason she put padlocks everywhere throughout the house. She would beat me with sticks and rulers. She would grab me by the hair and drag me around the house. These frightening, shattering happenings occurred frequently. (Some years later I learned she was suffering from mental disturbances.)

Because the home had become so terrifying, I would sometimes go home with my friends after school hours and stay as long as I dared. Other times I would go to the nearby seawall and gaze out at the ocean wishing I could jump into the waves. I seriously wondered if I bit my tongue hard enough, I could die by bleeding to death. I could not put myself into my studies at school. Whenever I talked with my mother, I was filled with tension and fear.

When I graduated from middle school, I was granted a school scholarship to a national nurses' school in the neighboring city of Kurume. My dorm fees and school tuition were paid by the scholarship. I was very grateful for this new arrangement.

While in nurses' training, I met a patient who was a Christian. She had her Bible laying beside her pillow. I knew nothing about the Bible, but for some reason I was awed by it. I could feel the spirit of calm and peace in this lady's life. My heart was searching for peace, but it seemed out of my reach.

After graduation from nurses' school, I went to Osaka (located five hundred miles from Omuta) to work in a hospital. For several years my life was very busy, but my heart was empty. I tried to get happiness by going to movies, hiking with friends, or learning to dance. Nothing brought me satisfaction.

I stayed in contact with my adoptive parents. I was told my mother's condition had become so serious she was put in a mental hospital. I made a quick trip back to Omuta to see if I could help my father in this difficult time. He declined my help.

While I was in Omuta for the short stay, I learned of a church there. A missionary, Leo Kaylor, was the pastor. I attended a few services and sensed the peace my heart was longing for. But I couldn't stay in Omuta for long. I had to return to my job in Osaka.

Upon returning to Osaka, I located the church I had been told about. It was in an old building, and the services were conducted in a large *tatami* (straw) mat room. Many *zabutons* (Japanese cushions for sitting on the floor) were lined up on the floor for people to sit on.

When I entered the room, there were several people sitting on the *zabutons* and praying loudly. It all seemed strange, but as I sat there, warmth filled my heart and tears came to my eyes.

I continued attending this church and came into a wonderful relationship with Jesus. I determined to follow Him all of my life. My life had been a dry and barren wilderness. Now God led me to abundant, well-watered pastures. Every day became a day of praise.

After I was baptized in water, I began to pray to be filled with the Holy Spirit. Many times at the end of services, I would go forward to pray for the baptism in the Holy Spirit. My heart was hungry for everything God had for me.

The following January 1969, I made another trip to Omuta to visit my parents for the New Year's holiday. I attended the New Year's conference at the Omuta church where Kaylor Sensei pastored. When the invitation was given for all who desired to be filled with the Holy Spirit to come forward, I responded.

Kaylor Sensei asked a lady praying near me if she would pray with me for the Holy Spirit. Very soon I began speaking in tongues. I wondered to myself, "Is this really the Holy Spirit?" The unknown words continued to gush forth, and I was overjoyed.

My life was transformed! After the New Year's holidays were over, I returned to Osaka to my work in the hospital. My life was filled with joy in those days, and I found it easy to talk to people about Christ.

A short time later, I met the man who later became my husband. He attended church and also accepted Jesus into his life. After he was saved, he never missed going to church. Later we were married. He was a very respectful husband. He loved the Lord and served in the church. He also did everything he could to help my adoptive parents.

The doctor had told me that I should not have children. However, I believed that God is the One Who gives life. God gave us three children. All three accepted Christ when they were in elementary school.

A feeling of responsibility toward my adoptive parents began stirring in me. By God's grace I could forget the past and the difficult times. Now I desired that they have the joy of salvation through Christ that my family and I experienced.

My husband and I moved our family back to Omuta in 1981 so we could be near my parents. We wanted to show them our love and to help them in any way we could. But ever since we had become Christians, my father had closed his heart to us. He treated us coldly. With disdain he would say, "Christianity is a foreign religion. In Japan we have Japanese religions."

Our family faithfully attended the Omuta Church where Kaylor Sensei was now assisting the Japanese pastor and conducting Bible training for young people.

A few years after our move to Omuta, my mother suddenly passed away. My father was lonely, but he didn't want to rely on anyone and kept himself aloof from us. Nonetheless, we reached out to him in every way we could.

At that time he asked me to take the responsibility of the daily care of his god-box. That would require that I burn incense, offer flowers, rice, and tea every morning in the worship of the dead spirits. I had to decline, explaining that as a Christian I could not do so. This greatly angered my father.

Shortly afterward, my father wrote in his will that "anyone who does not take care of the ancestral god-box, I do not consider them a child of mine." I was eliminated from his will.

As time passed my father, now eighty, began to fail physically. He needed our daily assistance, and we gladly poured our love upon him. Because of the loving care we showed my father in his sickness and need, he later re-wrote his will. He made it a very generous will toward me and my family.

My father's physical condition continued to worsen. After about a year, he was at death's door. At the very last, my husband and I stayed at his bedside caring for him. It seemed God had prepared his heart. I took a bold step and asked, "Father, won't you believe in Jesus?" He was too weak to speak, but he answered me by nodding his head, "Yes." His positive response took me by surprise. Since he was also hard of hearing, I thought perhaps he had misunderstood me. So just to check, I asked him, "Father, do you want something to drink?" He shook his head, "No!"

One more time I asked, "Father, do you believe in Jesus?" Again he nodded his head very emphatically, "Yes!" I knew he had responded to Jesus. That was an emotional moment for me.

It was 6:30 Sunday morning. We called Kaylor Sensei to come at once, as my father was near death. While we were waiting for him to arrive, my husband and I prayed and sang by my father's bedside,

> *"Yes, we'll gather at the River*
> *The beautiful, the beautiful River,*
> *Gather with the saints at the River,*
> *That flows from the Throne of God."*

When Kaylor Sensei arrived, he spoke to my father about Jesus. He quoted John 8:12, *"I am the light of the world. He who follows Me shall not walk in darkness but have the light of life."* My father was responding to Kaylor Sensei's guidance. A few hours later my father passed into the glories of heaven.

I had prayed for my father's salvation for such a long time. Now, at the very end of his life, he believed in Jesus and was saved. This is God's promise that, if we believe, our family will also be saved.

My husband and I are so happy to be planted in the newly formed Ariake Bible Church. When it came time to construct our church building, we were able to give from my father's estate toward the building needs. We did this with great rejoicing in the stead of my father. My husband and I praise God for all of His goodness to us and our family.

From Buddhism to Christ

By Kaneki Masuda
Written in 1998
(Translated by Leo Kaylor)

I am seventy-two years old and had been a devout Buddhist priest for forty years. I had done all the many ascetic practices of that religion: standing under cold water falls, sitting in Zen meditation in the snow and ice, all-night meditations, fastings, etc. Of the many sects of Buddhism, I had chosen to believe in the sect of the "fire-god." I believed it to be the most powerful.

In 1996 the doctor informed me I had cancer in my large intestine and in my liver. I felt like I had hit a blank wall. My mind was in total confusion and I was filled with great terror. The doctor operated and cut out two-thirds of my liver and part of my large intestine.

My daughter came from her home in far away Tochigi Prefecture to care for me. She was a Christian and for some time had talked to me about Christianity. But I had not given her a listening ear.

Two years passed and in March of 1998, the doctor told me the cancer had recurred in my liver. He advised that I have another operation as soon as possible. The university hospital had no available beds at that time, so I was put on a waiting list.

As I returned home from the doctor's office that day, my heart was filled with total darkness. I had no desire to eat. During the two weeks waiting for a bed at the hospital, I was totally alone in my mental suffering. It was living hell! I felt I could not cope with the utter despair I was in. I called my daughter and told her the cancer in my liver had recurred and that the doctor advised another operation.

During those miserable days of waiting for a hospital bed to open, I devoted myself to my Buddhist "fire-god" by worshiping in desperation at the Buddhist altar in my home. As a Buddhist priest, I had a larger altar than in most homes. There were many objects of worship. Others, who wished to do so, also came to my home to worship at my altar.

Out of the desperation of my feelings, I would kneel in front of the altar and beat the wooden drums which are used in Buddhist worship. I would beat those drums for three hours every morning and again for three hours every evening. I cried out in anguish and anger to the "fire-god." "I have so completely trusted in you. Now in my need, why don't you answer me?" I wanted to strike out in defiance against it. This living hell I was experiencing was terrible torment. I felt the terror of darkness and death.

After two weeks of mental agony and intense fear, I received a notice from the hospital. I would be admitted on April 14. The fear that I would never return to my home alive gripped me.

Early on the morning of April 14, I was out in front of my house waiting for a taxi. In my terrible state of mind, I was in a daze. For some reason I had an uneasy feeling I was forgetting something. I went back into my house in that foggy daze. At random I opened a desk drawer. There was the book *From Buddhism To Christ* my daughter had sent me. I had never read it. I put the book in my bag and went back outside to wait for the taxi.

At the hospital I checked into the room assigned me. It was a room with five other patients. After the evening meal, I was thinking that once I have the operation I won't feel like reading. So I began to read the book, *From Buddhism To Christ*.

The first half was about Buddhism. I already knew all that was written about my religion. Then the book suddenly changed to the story of Christ. I was totally ignorant of Christ. As I continued to read, I felt the depth of love in Christ's sacrifice of Himself for others. I was half-believing and half-doubting, wondering if these things could possibly be true. I couldn't put the book down and read all night long. It was time for breakfast the next morning when I finished the book.

My daughter arrived from Tochigi Prefecture on April 16 to be with me for the operation on the following day. She intended to stay with me for as long as I needed her. She spoke to me often about Christ and the Bible. But still my feelings about Buddhism hadn't changed. However, I so appreciated my daughter coming from so far away to be with me, I tried to listen politely to everything she said.

Finally my operation was on April 17. According to the doctor, they had taken out two-thirds of my liver in the first operation. All they could do this time was burn the cancerous area. I knew my condition was very serious.

A few days after the operation, my daughter said, "I have asked the pastor of Ariake Bible Church to come to see you here in the hospital. They are coming today." I was shocked! My image of a pastor was someone who is very stiff and solemn, dressed in a black garb with a black sash hanging down from around his waist, and holding a big, black book.

That afternoon the pastor and his wife entered my room. "Good afternoon! Hallelujah!" was their cheerful greeting. The pastor was a very large foreigner. I was shocked and my body became petrified.

The pastor was totally different than what I had imagined a pastor to be. He was gentle, smiling, and took my hand with his warm hand. His wife also spoke a warm greeting and gripped my hand firmly. I knew all five of the other patients in the room had their eyes glued on me and were taking it all in.

The pastor and his wife knew I was weak from the operation, so they stayed for just a short time. They talked to me about Christ. I felt nervous and everything seemed to go blank. He read from the Bible and then said, "Shall we pray; please repeat after me." I repeated the prayer in a weak, small voice, like the sound of a mosquito.

The pastor laid his hand on my back and prayed for my healing. That was the first time I had ever heard of "healing." He also told me that the brothers and sisters at the church were praying that I would soon recover. The pastor and his wife said they would come again; then they left.

I felt as if all my strength was suddenly drained out, and I relaxed. I didn't understand what "the brothers and sisters at church" meant. When I asked my daughter, she explained that was the term used for the other Christians. I also learned the pastor's name was Leo Kaylor.

Kaylor Sensei and his wife came again on April 30 and said, "Hallelujah! We've come again. You look like you are feeling better today. The brothers and sisters at church are praying every day for you." I had read in one of the books my daughter had given me, that, when someone is sick, the Christians pray for them. But to think that people would pray for someone they had never seen, caused a feeling of appreciation to well up in my heart. I was very thankful.

That day, again, the pastor and his wife were full of smiles, talked a short time about Jesus, read the Bible and prayed for me and for my healing, then left. They had even brought a beautiful arrangement of flowers for me. Hearing them say I was looking much better made me realize indeed I was gaining strength and getting better.

I was moved to a newly constructed section of the hospital on May 1. The room was spacious and bright with only three other patients. It was fourteen days after my operation and I had recovered enough to sit up in bed. Kaylor Sensei and his wife came to see me for the third time. They entered the new hospital room with smiling faces. I was sitting up in bed and I was the one to initiate the greeting. I reached out my hand and said, "Hallelujah!" As they smiled at me, I had an unspeakable, joyous feeling of close friendship well up within me.

Just then a nurse came in and kindly said to Kaylor Sensei and his wife, "I need to change Masuda San's bandage. Would you please step out and wait in the hall for a moment?" So Kaylor Sensei, his wife, and my daughter stepped out into the hallway. As the nurse was kneeling by my bed, she looked up at me and in her kind manner asked, "Masuda San, are you a Christian?" Without any hesitation, I said, "Yes, I'm a Christian!" "Well, that's great!" she said pleasantly, and then left the room.

Kaylor Sensei, his wife, and my daughter soon came back into the room. As they entered, clouds of mist seemed to billow from the ceiling and filled the room. Then it cleared away. I told them about the conversation with the nurse and they rejoiced with me.

When Kaylor Sensei and his wife left, I told my daughter I had made a firm decision to follow Christ. I had found my way and made up my mind. She exclaimed, *"Hona kotsu ka, Otoosan?"* (local dialect meaning "Do you really mean it, Father?"). She rejoiced with me. My heart was filled with light and peace. "I will not look back, but will press on ahead" was the strong vow I made in my heart. I was changing, gaining strength, and my heart was getting brighter all the time. Every day my daughter talked further with me about Christ and I gladly listened.

Kaylor Sensei and his wife continued to visit me. They brought Yamato San and his wife from the church and introduced them to me. I expressed my decision to follow Jesus and they rejoiced. I was happy to learn the Yamatos lived in Omuta in a neighborhood near mine. In fact, they knew exactly where my house was since it was well known in that neighborhood as a place of worshiping the "fire-god."

The doctors were pleased with my speedy recovery. I was told I could leave the hospital on May 21. My daughter took me home and stayed for a number of weeks to care for me.

Now the big task was to rid my house of all the idols and articles of worship I had served so long. My daughter was intent to clean my house of every single article connected with my former way of worship. The house was filled with many things. My daughter made a big pile of everything she could find. She did a thorough job.

Kaylor Sensei and some of the people from the church came to remove all the Buddhist paraphernalia from my house. It was enough stuff to fill two vans. Then Kaylor Sensei and some of the Christians came and walked through my home anointing it with oil. They prayed for my house to be cleansed from all evil powers.

A few days later, I attended Sunday morning worship at the church. It was the first time I had ever been in a church. I didn't know the songs, but I tried to sing. Everything was totally new to me. At the end of the service, many people came to shake hands and greeted me warmly. I could feel their love. These were the people who had been praying for me.

May 31, 1998, was the most memorable day of my life. I was baptized in water on that day. Jesus was my Savior, the Light of Life. I was so happy.

I want to thank my daughter, Yoko, who loved me and guided me to Christ's salvation. Also from deep in my heart, I want to thank Kaylor Sensei and his wife. They opened up the things of Christ to me and led me. I want to thank all the Christians who prayed for me. Hallelujah, Praise the Lord!

June 15, 1998

Masuda San (left) and Yamato San worshipping in a church service

Meeting Again after Forty-five Years *(by Leo)*

It was over forty-five years ago in 1960, when Nishinami San (age twenty-six) accepted Christ. This was during our first few years of pioneering the Omuta Church.

One morning, when Nishinami San opened his morning newspaper, a gospel tract fell out onto the floor. We had some ten thousand gospel tracts inserted in that morning's newspapers for distribution throughout our area. Nishinami San's attention was drawn to the words on the tract, *"Come to me all you who labor and are heavy laden, and I will give you rest." Matthew 11:28.* His heart was prepared to respond to God's Word.

Soon after receiving the tract, Nishinami San found our home and attended a Sunday night service. At the close of my message, I asked those who wished to believe in Jesus to raise their hand. His

The Omuta group at summer camp meeting, August 1960.
Nishinami San is at center with Bible. Robby (5), front. Leo holding
Steven (1½), Phyllis holding Nathan (5 months)

hand went up saying, "Yes, I believe in Jesus." He told us he was filled with an indescribable peace.

Nishinami San began attending Sunday night services faithfully. His job required him to work Sunday mornings. He gladly helped us in our street evangelism of passing out tracts. Nishinami San was among our group of Christians who went to the summer camp meetings at Kirishima in August 1960. In obedience to Christ, he was baptized in water at that time.

Nishinami San attended our church for only seven months. The construction company for which he worked transferred him to their next building project in another city. We lost contact with Nishinami San after that. He seemed to be such a promising young man. Through the years I had thought from time to time, "I wonder whatever happened to Nishinami San?"

Recently, I was talking with Nishida Sensei at the Fukuoka Harvest Church. He said to me, "Kaylor Sensei, the other Sunday in our church we had two men from the Gideon Bible Society give a presentation of their work to our church. One of the men had commented that a missionary by the name of Leo Kaylor in Omuta had led him to Christ many years ago. Do you remember—let's see, what was his name?"

I quickly asked, "You don't mean Nishinami San, do you?" "Yes, that's it," Nishida Sensei responded. I was astounded! A couple weeks later on a Thursday afternoon, Nishida Sensei made arrangements for Nishinami San and his wife to come to his church. Phyllis and I drove to Fukuoka to meet them there.

It was a wonderful time of reunion after some forty-five years. Nishinami San told me, "I have desired in my heart to see you just one more time before Jesus takes me home to heaven."

All those many years ago when we first met Nishinami San, he was always a well-groomed young man. Now we were talking with a well-groomed, silver-haired gentleman of seventy-two years. We spent nearly two hours talking together about God's many blessings in our lives during those intervening years.

Nishinami San told us that through the years, wherever he was located, he always found a local church and attended faithfully. He is now retired and is an elder in a church in Fukuoka. He is also an active member of the Gideon Bible Society.

What a tremendous example of the good seed of the gospel falling upon good ground and bringing forth an abundant harvest.

After forty-five years we met Nishinami San once again, with his wife.

Leafing through Life's Pages *(by Phyllis)*

Memories are wonderful. We can leaf through life's pages and remember happenings of many years gone by. The older we get, the more pages we have to leisurely leaf through and see God's loving Hand guiding our lives.

Why did I want to be a missionary? God was printing it on the pages of my life from the time I was very young. Leafing through the pages, I come across specific times when missionaries had a profound effect on me.

The earliest I can remember was while our family still lived at Hay, Washington. A missionary family to Indonesia by the name of Patterson had made an impact upon my life. They had told of their missionary experiences in the little, white church at Hay. The missionaries, who had a girl about my age, also spoke at the public school's student body assembly. I sat in that assembly among the other second graders.

Through the years I had wished I could have the opportunity to see that missionary family again and tell them how they had impacted me as a little girl. I had heard that some of the Patterson family were in Bethel Temple church in Seattle, but an opportunity to meet them never came about.

Until—

In 2004 Bethel Temple merged with The City Church in Seattle, which is pastored by Wendell and Gini Smith. At their invitation Leo and I had the privilege of going to Seattle and attending their Global Strategy Conference in May 2006.

One evening during the conference, Leo and I were standing in the cafeteria line for the evening meal. A couple about our age was passing through the same line. Someone nearby mentioned to us that this couple, Bob and Marian Brodland, was from the former Bethel Temple church. They were missionaries to Indonesia.

My mind churned fast. Could it be? We started up a conversation with them. "Do you know the W. W. Pattersons?" "Yes," she replied, "he was my father." The answer I was looking for came so suddenly I was stunned!

Then question after question spilled out. "Do you know where the little town of Hay is?" (I could ask one hundred people if they know where Hay, Washington, is and likely one hundred people would answer, "No.") She replied again, "Yes, I went there with my parents when I was a little girl. We visited the church in Hay during furloughs in 1939 and 1941."

More of our mutual past unfolded as we sat down together for the evening meal. We were sharing from the same pages of life's book. Marian Brodland told me, "My mother's father was an evangelist and a carpenter. He built that little church in Hay."

(My grandfather, Papa, had donated the land and provided the funds for the building.)

The four of us reminisced on and on. I don't think any of us were aware of the good food we were eating. Marian and I were in awe to be pointing back to the same pages of life where our paths had crossed.

God had been mindful of my desire to someday meet someone of the Patterson family. God arranged it for me. No one else could have done so.

God in Our Daily Lives

God seems to take pleasure in unexpectedly stepping into our daily lives. When the gracious Hand of the Lord comes upon us in those unexpected times and places, it helps us to realize how much He cares for us.

Here is another such incident:

For some years Leo had a reclining chair that was a favorite of his for relaxing. Through the years it began wearing down with age. Wire proved successful in making repairs on a number of occasions. But knowing Leo's chair was on its "last leg," we would periodically stop by furniture stores to see what would be available to replace it. Finally the breakdown of the old chair was such that another piece of wire just wasn't enough to put it into any kind of working condition. We decided Leo needed a new chair.

The search was on. All the reclining chairs we had seen in our occasional searching were much too big and plush to bring into our 12' x 12' room. That room already accommodated a small sofa, the TV, a bookcase, the dining room table with its chairs, and a china cabinet. Finding the right chair in the right size of the right color at the right price was a challenge.

One day we set out to face that challenge intending to search every furniture store within a reasonable radius. An hour's drive wasn't too far if that were necessary.

Just a short distance from where we live was a roadside furniture store. That was our first stop. As usual the reclining chairs were too big, too expensive, and too gaudy in color. Color was an important factor to me. What I lacked in musical talent, I seemed to have in coordinating colors and design. I love the harmony that colors can create when they compliment one another. Isn't the same true with us—harmony is created when we verbally compliment one another!

That day while looking at the reclining chairs in the nearby furniture store, something I had never before seen in Japan caught my eye. A sofa hide-a-bed was on display. I couldn't believe my eyes, but there it was. I drew Leo's attention to it.

A clerk saw our interest in the sofa hide-a-bed. He came to show us how great this new invention was. With some difficulty he tried to figure out how to slide the bed back into the sofa. We stood silently by as though we knew nothing about how that "new invention" worked! The clerk continued to tell us all the marvels of this piece of furniture. Then he added, "We got this sofa in our store just a few days ago."

The size was right, the color was right, and the price was right. We purchased it. Not long after that, the furniture store went out of business.

That "new invention" has been a pleasure to us for several years now. Leo very comfortably lounges on the sofa. God's thoughts were so far above ours. How much better a reasonably sized sofa for our limited space, than a huge, plush recliner that would suffice for only one person. And with the sofa came a comfortable hide-a-bed, something we had never thought possible in Japan. Nor have we ever seen another such sofa on display in any store since then.

The story goes on. A few years after we purchased our sofa with the comfortable hide-a-bed, we were in the U.S. for a short stay. One day I just happened (No! God arranged it!) to overhear some ladies discussing how uncomfortable hide-a-beds are. One of the ladies made a statement that jolted me to attention, "There is only one hide-a-bed I ever slept on that was comfortable. It was a Sears product made in Canada."

That is exactly what our hide-a-bed is, a Sears product made in Canada! God ordered it from Canada, shipped it to Japan, and sent it way down to the southern part of Japan to a roadside furniture store very near us. We are convinced He did it for us. It didn't just happen.

Tributes, Memories, and Daddy's Passing

A Tribute to My Parents *(by Leo)*

My father and mother had returned to the U.S. from their missionary work in India in 1929. I was born two years later. From my earliest memories, our family was always in church on Sunday mornings, Sunday evenings and Wednesday nights. I learned to love the House of God.

During the years I was growing up in Sulphur Springs, Arkansas, times were hard and my parents experienced many financial difficulties. They usually kept two or three cows for milking. The cream was separated from the milk by a hand-cranked separator and sold to a creamery. They raised fryer chickens for meat and hens for laying eggs. Daddy worked at various jobs of construction or whatever he could do to help with their financial needs.

My parents never complained of our lack of material things, but always prayed and trusted God to supply our daily needs. When the supply came—sometimes in very unusual ways—they would rejoice in God's Hand of blessing upon us. This was excellent training for me. I would learn to use those same principles of trusting God during hard times in my own missionary career.

My mother was a great intercessor and prayed much for us children. She literally went into her prayer closet and prayed to the Father in secret, and the Father certainly did reward her openly. It was also from my mother I learned the value of memorizing the Scriptures.

My father was a diligent student of the Word and a wonderful Bible teacher. He was the main source of my Bible school training—I learned much from him.

After I entered the University of Arkansas, my parents moved to Ozark, Arkansas, and became teachers at the newly formed Ozark Bible Institute. Daddy was one of their main Bible teachers for a number of years. Many young people were trained under his teaching.

My mother passed away in June 1952, at the age of sixty-two. This was just six months after I left for Japan. My father retired from Bible school teaching and, after marrying again, moved back to Sulphur Springs. He continued to be active until the age of eighty-two, when God summoned him, in 1966, to a higher calling to receive his heavenly reward.

I am so grateful for my godly parents and for the tremendous spiritual heritage I have received from them. Their faith and their prayers have followed me these many years.

More Memories of Daddy and Mama *(by Phyllis)*

My father, Everett Poe, was everyone's friend. He loved God with a passion, loved his family, and loved life. He was a weather-worn son of the soil who loved the great outdoors.

I have pleasant memories of rainy days when I was a small child. When Daddy couldn't work outside, he sometimes would bring the large circular blade from his motorized wood saw into our spacious kitchen. Daddy used the saw for cutting up wood for our stoves—the kitchen stove and the majestic looking "German Heater" in the living room.

As Daddy painstakingly filed the jagged edge of the large circular blade, he would sing some of his favorite hymns with a jolly good spirit. His cheerfulness would fill the room. He only knew a few lines of each song and he would sing those lines over and over.

"There'll be no dark valley when Jesus comes, there'll be no dark valley when Jesus comes, there'll be no dark valley...." Those words still ring

in my heart. To me Daddy's singing was great. Rainy days, even now, command some kind of warmth in my heart because of those childhood memories.

Fishing was one of Daddy's greatest pleasures. He was a very diligent worker, so he was only able to take time for fishing now and then. When Daddy went fishing, he never went alone. He would share his pleasure with family or friends. He wanted everyone to enjoy life as he did and to him fishing was one of the sources of a great life. In later years Daddy would jokingly chuckle, "The time a man spends fishing isn't counted in his age."

I am joining Daddy in one of his greatest pleasures.

Mama was the best of mothers. All her interests centered in her family. She gave herself unreservedly to whatever our needs were and loved us in that same unreserved manner.

Mama, like Daddy, loved the outdoors. She was a great companion to Daddy in fishing and hunting. We children were usually taken with them on those wonderful excursions.

Mama believed in discipline. If discipline were necessary, it was discipline with a purpose. I well remember one of those incidents. On that particular occasion, as a strong-willed little girl, I was letting it be known I wasn't happy about something. I have no memory of what that something was. To put some emphasis into my unhappy feelings, I carried on in a full-blown tantrum—screaming, thrashing, and dancing in the middle of the floor. It was what happened next that implanted this incident in my memory.

Mama didn't appear very moved by my actions until the storm calmed a bit. Then, with a switch in her hand, she informed me there was going to be a replay of what had just been so dramatically performed. I was instructed to get back into the middle of the floor and carry on again with the same screaming, thrashing, and dancing using the same volume and same high-spirited effort. Mama, with the switch in her hand, decided how long the replay would run. That was the last time Mama had to deal with a tantrum by her strong-willed little girl. I dearly loved and respected Mama for the great mother she was.

Daddy and Mama pointed us to the Almighty God. Their lives and faith were genuine. Three of us four children went into the ministry. Grandchildren were greatly impacted by Grandpa and Grandma Poe's love for God. They, too, set their own footsteps upon the High Way that Grandpa and Grandma walked.

Daddy Enters the Glories of Heaven

Daddy was seventy-three when Mama passed away in 1975. Daddy wasn't one to just sit in his sorrow and loneliness. He busied himself with the many things that interested him. He visited us in Japan on a number of occasions. At one time he spent a whole year with us. Many Japanese loved Daddy and endearingly called him *Poe Ojiisan* (Grandpa Poe). Daddy also enjoyed spending time with my brother, Sam, and his family who were missionaries in Mexico at that time.

Daddy continued a relatively active life until he was nearly ninety-two. Then we increasingly noticed the sparkle of life fading. Pleasures weren't pleasures any longer, not even fishing. His memory began to fade.

My brother Paul and his wife Joan took Daddy into their home and gave him the best of care. They spoke of it as a privilege. We all knew it was a great challenge to care for our failing Daddy with all of his many needs. The love Paul and Joan poured upon him was very pleasing to God.

Several times during Daddy's last few years, Leo sent me home just to be near him for a few days. Other times we went together. The time came when Daddy didn't seem to recognize me anymore, but still I wanted to be near him.

Daddy continued to weaken, and we knew his sojourn on earth would soon be over. Again, Leo and I made the trip to the U.S. and went to Paul's where Daddy was. One morning Paul, Joan, Leo, and I were having devotions together in their living room. We were singing some hymns as we often did on such occasions. Daddy sat quietly with bowed head in a special chair Paul had arranged for him. Daddy seldom opened his tired eyes, seldom spoke, and seldom showed much response to life.

That morning one of the hymns we sang was *Blessed Assurance*. Every phrase is a triumphant proclamation. Hearing the song must have sparked some memory in Daddy. When we finished the hymn, Daddy opened his eyes wide, and with feeling he said, "This is my song, this is my song!" For a moment, Daddy was back with us. Our emotions were deeply stirred.

One week later on March 2, 1996, at the age of ninety-four, Daddy dropped his worn out robe of flesh. He took flight to the glories of heaven—glories he had glimpses of during his long walk with God.

Daddy's home-going service radiated his deep faith in Almighty God. It was a celebration of a life lived in harmony with his Savior. *Blessed Assurance* was sung in honor of Daddy's recent proclamation. We also sang one of Daddy's favorite hymns, *"All hail the power of Jesus Name, let angels prostrate fall...."* When Daddy was moved with

Daddy, a man of unshakable faith in his God

a heart full of praise to his God, he would often spontaneously and emphatically proclaim those words, wherever he might be.

The rich spiritual heritage we received from Daddy and Mama

Nine grandsons solemnly and proudly carry their grandpa's casket to its final resting place.

is shared by four children, twenty-three grandchildren, and forty-three great-grandchildren (at the time of Daddy's departure). Many more great-grandchildren were added in later years.

I wrote the following poem for Daddy in 1991.

You Are So Genuine, You Are So Real

On the eighteenth of March, 19-0-2,
God smiled on this day with what He would do.
A son He set free from the young mother's womb,
Which brought joy overflowing to that homesteader's home.
   Joy so genuine.   Joy so real.

Eighteen good years passed upon the lad's life,
A carefree young lad, yet within there was strife.
A longing to meet Jesus was deep in his soul,
And Jesus did meet him at the old tent pole.
          Life became genuine.   Life became real.

Many more years were added to his days,
Four grown children with children to raise,
Each with an eye on Daddy and Grand-dad,
On a life lived in harmony which he learned as a lad.
          Daddy so genuine.   Daddy so real.

When motherhood problems would frustrate my day,
I sometimes asked, "Daddy, what do you say?"
Your answer was simple; it came from your soul,
A truth you had learned at the old tent pole,
          "Simply be genuine.   Simply be real."

Thank you, dear Daddy, for showing us the way,
In all that you do and all that you say.
We've seen your example, and all of us feel—
          You are so genuine.   You are so real.

I wrote the following poem for Daddy's ninetieth birthday in 1992. It's of an incident that happened when I was a child.

With Pitcher In Hand

It was a hot, sultry night in summertime Hay,
And upstairs the old house was doubly that way.
Zella was sleeping on her half the bed;
The middle was a line, we had both clearly said.

I drifted to sleep on that hot summer night;
No need for the lantern—it was still a bit light.
But sleep wasn't sound as I tumbled and tossed,
Careful even in my sleep that the line wasn't crossed.

Much later I awoke, and my throat was so dry;
For Mama to help me, how I wanted to cry.
For it was Mama who brought to us water in the night,
And Mama who helped us, no matter the plight.

Zella still sleeping in a comfortable heap,
And I drifted again into some kind of sleep.

Then there you were, Daddy, with pitcher in hand;
Not far from my bedside so tall you did stand.
The water you carried did sparkle and gleam;
And then I awoke—it was only a dream.

I've pondered that dream with the passing of time.
Its meaning to me is very sublime.

It was from you, dear Daddy, with pitcher in hand,
That we received water from God's Promised Land;
Crystal clear water that flows from the Throne,
And all who partake do become God's own.

Thank you, dear Daddy, for standing so tall—
With pitcher in hand, you've given to all.

Expressions from Our Children

Ministering Together as a Family

Robert Kaylor

It was my first "ministry trip." I was only eight years old. Dad had been invited to minister on the island of Yakushima and decided to take me along. I was so excited I could hardly sleep the night before. The long trip included a middle-of-the-night train ride and then six hours on a ferry the next morning. Not only was it an extended time alone with Dad, but also an exposure of doing "ministry together." For me it was the first of many ministry trips and opportunities involving Dad and me and my brothers and sisters. Sometimes it would be all of us together as a family; at other times just one or two of us alone would join Dad or my parents for various ministry opportunities.

Church and ministry together was always a family affair. There were times we would go out as a family for street meetings. Dad would play his trombone; Mom, the accordion; and I played the guitar while we sang, *"Would you be free from your burden of sin, there is power in the blood"* or other evangelistic songs. Then Dad would give a short message or someone would share a testimony as the rest of us passed out gospel tracts. As we grew older, we were given opportunities in the church to lead worship, share a testimony or give a short gospel message. We were also actively involved in other areas in the church. In this way we cut our teeth in ministry and grew up feeling and being a part of the church ministry team.

As the years went by, these experiences gave me a taste and hunger to be involved in full-time ministry. With this background, as a teenager I began to seriously seek God about my future and

Rob on his first ministry trip with his Dad, 1963

what He would have me do with my life. When the Lord spoke very clearly, calling me to full time service in His work, I responded enthusiastically with great joy. That calling has kept me going through all my years of ministry.

Thanks, Dad and Mom, for your example and heart of service in the Kingdom of God and for including us in the work of the ministry from as far back as I can remember. You laid a very wonderful foundation in my life, for which I am very grateful. And it is a great privilege to work together side-by-side in the ministry even to this day.

My Greatest Inheritance

Steven Kaylor

I often tell people that the greatest inheritance that has been given to me is my upbringing and the faith of my parents. As I read the manuscript for *Unto A Land That I Will Show You*, I relived the many stories and events that we were privileged to witness as part of our lives. I am again overwhelmed at the amazing grace of God that has been poured out on our family. For sure, there are no material riches or earthly possessions that can compare to the wealth that our parents invested in us.

Those that know my parents would agree that they are some of the most cheerful and positive people you will meet. Their positive attitudes are certainly some of the greatest aspects of the heritage that I received from them. I would like to share three things that I have especially observed in their lives.

First, my parents were always positive about Japan and the Japanese people. I never remember them saying anything negative about the culture, food, or people. They have truly loved Japan and it has showed in all that they do. I know this is one reason why the Japanese so love and honor them.

Second, my parents were always positive about the ministry and what the Lord would do. They often spoke of the great things they believed God had planned for this nation. They considered serving the Lord in Japan a wonderful privilege. I am so thankful for such a positive and faith-filled environment that was always a part of our home and our church.

Third, my parents were always positive about the family. Mondays were family days. They were very creative and saw to it that we had fun-filled days of adventure and excitement. We were also included in the many ministry activities they were involved in. I never felt neglected or sacrificed because of the ministry. I am sure that the rest of my siblings would also say that the things

Steven and Nathan, with Rusty, in their straw creation

we did together as a family are some of our greatest childhood memories.

Our parents, Leo and Phyllis Kaylor, are our pride and joy. Each one of us six children is delighted that their book has been written. Our parents' story is now available for many to read and enjoy. I know that everyone reading this book will find their lives enriched by what is also my greatest inheritance.

The Japan Advantage

Nathan Kaylor

I consider it an honor to have been born into a missionary family and to have been raised on the mission field. Whenever I am asked, "Where were you born?" or "Where did you grow up?" I am able to reply, almost boastfully, "I was born in Japan and grew up there." The usual reaction to that is something like "Wow! That must have been interesting." Yes. As a matter of fact, it was. There are a number of things that made growing up in Japan unique and interesting. Here are just some of the things I experienced as a result of being raised in a missionary family in a foreign land.

1. *I am bilingual.* All of us kids learned Japanese while growing up and playing with other children. At home we mostly spoke English. Sometimes it was easier to express ourselves using both languages. Being bilingual gave us an unfair advantage when playing with other kids. When playing with the Japanese, we could communicate secretly in English; when playing with kids in the U.S., we would communicate in Japanese. Maybe that wasn't very fair for us to do, but, hey, we were missionary kids! We had advantages others didn't.

2. *Living in a different culture and lifestyle.* There are so many things about Japan that are unique—the people, the food, the culture. I have been enriched by the fact that these are some of the fabrics that make up who I am.

3. *Proclaiming the gospel message to those who have never heard of it.* My parents made it a point to involve the whole family in reaching the Japanese with the gospel. I can remember from an early age standing on a street corner and passing out gospel tracts to those passing by while we had what we called "street meetings." We spent countless hours canvassing neighborhoods or standing outside of schools passing out tracts and inviting people to special evangelistic meetings. Many times Daddy would take us with him when he went to visit someone in their home or at the hospital. As young children, most of the time we went knowing that we would be the recipient of a little snack of some kind from the person we were visiting.

4. *We received "special treatment."* We had blonde hair, blue eyes, and "white" skin. It was hard to miss us in a crowd, especially since we lived in rural Japan where we were the only foreigners (*gaijin*).

Helping Nathan hit the mark.
Croquet was a family favorite for Monday fun.

Often it was the first time for some of them to see a *gaijin* in person. Little grandmothers at grocery stores would ask Mama if they could touch our "golden" hair. Total strangers would come up and want to use their limited English on us to see if we could understand what they were saying. It was almost like having a celebrity status. I can remember as a little boy being allowed on the bridge of a big ferry boat while on one of our trips to or from Yakushima. Occasionally, we were even allowed to take the helm for a while. No other passengers were allowed on the bridge.

5. *Mondays were Family Fun Days.* Since we were homeschooled, my parents were in charge of our schedule. Therefore, Mondays were designated as "Family Fun Day." We did our schoolwork Tuesday through Saturday. We always looked forward to Mondays, whether it was going to the beach to look for exotic seashells or as simple as going to a park for a picnic. Regardless of what else was going on in the ministry or the church, we could always count on doing something fun on Mondays.

6. *Quality time with ministers.* We had the opportunity to meet and spend quality time with many top-notch ministers who would come to our church from time to time. Occasionally, they would even stay in our home and eat meals at our table. Whether it was Mama's homemade waffles for breakfast or a late-night snack after church, the times sitting around our table with these men and women of God were a highlight for us kids, making many pleasant memories.

Yes, it truly was a privilege to have grown up in Japan. Being part of such a wonderful missionary family is an honor. It is with a grateful heart that I would like to thank my parents for heeding the call of God to go to Japan. It has made a huge difference in my life, for sure!

Memories of Japan

Joyce Kaylor Robinson

Japan brings back many memories for me. When people find out that I had lived in Japan, they will often ask me, "What was it like growing up there?" or "Wasn't it different to live there?" Yes, compared to the U.S., everything is different in Japan—the food, the people, the language, the culture, the houses, and even the smells and sounds. But to my brothers, sister, and me, living in Japan was normal. I was privileged to have experienced things that a typical American would not experience.

The two years we lived in Yakushima when I was seven and eight were probably the highlight of my childhood. The boat trip of four hours always seemed like an eternity when the seas were rough. It was always a relief when we could see the outline of the island off in the distance.

In the small village where we lived, we had a lot of fun roaming the narrow streets and swimming in the Ambo River near our house, as well as playing on the sandy beaches. I still have a number of shells that we found there. We lived on the second floor above the kindergarten facilities and enjoyed interacting with the children during the day. I remember frequently riding in the kindergarten vans that took the children home in the afternoons.

Hiking into the mountains to see the huge Yakusugi (cedar trees) remains a vivid memory. It was also there in Yakushima that my brothers Steven and Nathan and I were water baptized in the cold ocean water. There are only a few places in the world as beautiful as Yakushima, and I am fortunate to have experienced this as part of my childhood.

When I graduated from high school, my parents suggested that I spend an extra year in Japan before going to Portland Bible College. I spent that year helping in the kindergarten on Yakushima in the little village of Onoaida. Even though it was not

Skating with Joyce on our ice skating day

the same village that we lived in several years previously, it was still the same beautiful island, and it still took four hours by ferry to get there! I lived with the Takeshita family who had operated the kindergarten for many years. The Takeshitas have become like family to all of us.

I left Japan the spring of 1981 and have returned to visit there several times. I had the privilege of going with my husband, Gary, the same year we were married in 1989. Several years later we had another opportunity to visit Japan with our family of three boys in 1998. I also took my youngest son, Kevin, for my parents' fiftieth ministry anniversary in 2002. Each time I returned to visit, the sights, sounds, and smells of my childhood come flooding back. Nothing can erase those memories.

A Scripture comes to mind that describe my parents' life in Japan: *"Trust in the Lord with all your heart, and lean not on your own understanding; in all your ways acknowledge Him, and He shall direct your paths." Proverbs 3:5,6*

They both trusted in God when they went separately to Japan, and they trusted in God through every challenge and decision that they faced. Each time, God was faithful to direct their paths. Now, when we face our own challenges, Gary and I have turned to my parents many times. They have encouraged and prayed with us regarding our challenges or decisions and have given their words of wisdom. What an honor to have wonderful godly parents. Gary and I love you very much!

Eagle Parents

Joel Kaylor

I have many fond memories of growing up in Japan. One of the highlights was times spent on the beach near our home. Mama put together incredible wiener roasts, and I frequently found a baseball among the debris that collected on the beach. Because of my endless supply of baseballs from our beach trips, I never had to buy any while growing up—what else could I ask for?

I will never forget the countless times when our family walked the sandy beach praying and seeking God's will, particularly when Daddy and Mama were facing important decisions. It seemed as though a full moon would come out on so many of those evenings. Mama would always say that it symbolized God's full blessing and faithfulness. To this day, each time I see a full moon I am reminded of God's blessings and faithfulness.

Another childhood memory was outlining a Christmas tree of green garland on the wall. Real Christmas trees were not available, but Daddy and Mama always found ways to make any occasion special!

Joel and Melodee looking for small edible snails, a delicacy of the Japanese, during one of our days at the Tamana River

One reason why I have so many special memories is because Daddy and Mama always included Melodee and me in everything they did. Even though they were very busy with church activities, I never felt neglected. On the contrary I knew I was important to them and I was loved. They used every opportunity to make themselves available to me. Those opportunities were little decisions they made to invest in me which helped me wisely make the bigger decisions in life. To this day they are a constant source of love, encouragement, support, reassurance, and guidance.

When I was fourteen, the four of us took an overnight ferry to attend a pastors' conference. The speaker gave an altar call one night for the young people to commit to full time ministry. I did not want to go into the ministry but felt pressure to respond. I felt that if I did not respond I would disappoint Daddy and Mama. To get that off of my chest, I leaned over to Mama who was standing next to me and whispered, "I don't think I will go up." Without missing a beat—and she never misses a beat—Mama put her arms around me and whispered back, "That's great! Whatever God has for you is what Daddy and I want for you." I felt like a bird set free from a cage! It was a relief to know that they would support me, even if I didn't go into the ministry.

A few years later at a youth camp, I had a powerful encounter with God. He spoke to me in no uncertain terms that I was to minister in Japan. I responded in faith to this call. I committed myself to ministry, not because of my parents' desire, nor was I trying to be like someone else, but because that was God's call on my life.

I am convinced that the reason I sincerely responded to God was because Daddy and Mama never pressured me into the ministry. They just wanted God's best for me. They had modeled obedience to God's call on their lives, and I was simply following their example—responding to my calling.

God gave me the perfect wife, Kelly McClenahan, who also had a personal calling to Japan. Together, with our children, we are now pursuing our ministry to the Japanese people.

Thank you, Daddy and Mama, for always being there for me and showing me what it means to fully trust, obey, and follow Christ. In honor of you and what I learned from you, I dedicate the following:

Eagle Parents

(Written December 2000)

Eagle parents strategically build a safe place to raise their children.

Eagle parents go to great lengths to provide for their children even in the midst of danger.

Eagle parents know how to wait for the breeze, soar in the wind, and fly high in the sky.

Eagle parents use their keen eyesight to protect, provide, and teach their children.

Eagle parents are always able to renew their strength.

Eagle parents are not afraid to let their children fly on their own, but are always there for support.

Eagle parents pass on their inheritance of great parenting.

Thank you, Daddy and Mama, for being Eagle Parents.

Melodee, Leo, and Joel sitting in a tropical tree in Yakushima during one of our many trips there

Daddy and Mama Impacted My Life

Melodee Kaylor Barnhart

From the time I was a young girl, I watched Daddy and Mama in their personal relationship with God. It made a significant impact on me. They would read their Bibles and pray together every morning, each encouraging the other with special insight.

One Sunday when I was about twelve years old, I remember Daddy exhorting the congregation to use the daily reading plan to read through the Bible in one year. Having seen Daddy and Mama's genuine examples, I was challenged to begin.

When I had questions about things I was reading in the Bible, I would write them down and ask Daddy. On occasion I interrupted his diligent studies, but he would patiently answer my questions. Daddy always enjoyed talking about the Bible.

Mama often said the full moon was a reminder of God's full blessing shining down on us. I specifically remember one furlough trip to the U.S. Daddy, Mama, Joel, and I were waiting to board our plane at Tokyo. Mechanical problems on the plane had delayed our departure. The hour was late and there were concerns we may not be able to fly that night.

During our late-night waiting in the airport, Mama suddenly saw a magnificent, full moon shining through the windows. She proclaimed, "That is God reminding us of His full blessings on our furlough." Shortly the mechanical problem was fixed. All waiting passengers boarded the plane and we departed for the U.S.

Whenever I see a full moon, I am reminded of Mama's stead-fastness in proclaiming God's blessings instead of concentrating on negative circumstances. Mama always says, "Trust God. He will guide you." Mama made God real in life.

Whenever we as a family faced difficulties or an unknown, Daddy and Mama had us kids join them in prayer. Daddy and Mama were always faithful to seek God's will.

Thank you for imparting the love of the Scriptures and for reminding us of God's blessings.

Daddy and Mama, I am proud to say, "...*you are so genuine. You are so real.*"

And the Journey Goes on

Leo and I each had separately said, "Here I am, Lord. Send me." That was 1951. Leo left for Japan by ship in December 1951. I went, also by ship, in May 1952.

One year later, 1953, by God's sovereign Hand upon our lives, we were married. We've walked the journey together since then, and a marvelous journey it has been. The gracious Hand of the Lord has been upon us all the way.

God, in His sovereignty, brings His children to renewed consecration to His will any number of times along the journey. Times of discouragement, times of problems, times of testing—all are times when we must cling to the Lord our God and again say, "Yes, Lord. My faith is in You alone. Nothing matters but Your will." He comes alongside and touches us with His gracious Hand of love. Our spirits are renewed and we happily press on.

Since Leo and I have been on the journey all these many years, the question now is often asked "When are you going to retire?" I have mused in my heart, "God, You told Noah when to go into the ark. You also told him when to leave the ark. You clearly called Leo and me to Japan. I firmly believe You will just as clearly tell us when our journey in Japan is completed."

Until then Leo and I shall joyfully continue on in our journey. Our spirits are constantly being renewed, and we press on with rejoicing.

A Final Word *(by Leo)*

We are living in very momentous days. While the nations of the world are in great turmoil and confusion, this is the greatest hour of opportunity for God's people to align themselves with the purposes of God.

God's purpose is for the nations to hear the gospel. However, there are yet many people groups throughout the nations with no gospel witness.

Jesus said:

> *"The harvest truly is plentiful, but the laborers are few"* (Matthew 9:37).
>
> *"Behold, I say to you, lift up your eyes and look at the fields, for they are already white for harvest"* (John 4:35).
>
> *"And this gospel of the kingdom will be preached in all the world as a witness to all the nations, and then the end will come"* (Matthew 14:14).

In these days of unprecedented opportunity to be a part of the great end-time harvest of souls, every person who loves the Lord can find a place of effective service for God.

In the story of Gideon and his three hundred, the Scripture says, *"Every man stood in his place..."* (Judges 7:21).

May each one of us stand in our place, fully dedicated to God's purpose for our life. There is no greater joy and fulfillment than this!

Glossary

Benjo	Obsolete Japanese word—toilet, outhouse
Dubs	American slang—to lay claim to
Gaijin	Japanese word—foreigner
Geta	Japanese wooden clogs
Gunnysack	A coarse sack made of burlap; used for sacking wheat
Prefecture	A geographical designation equivalent to state or province
San	Japanese word added to the end of a person's name—Mr., Mrs., or Miss
Sensei	Japanese word—teacher. It is used widely for anyone who teaches anything.
Tit for tat	A situation in which you do something bad to someone, because they have done the same to you.
Zabuton	Japanese cushion for sitting on the floor.

We trust that you enjoyed the book.
We would love to hear from you.

Leo and Phyllis

Leo & Phyllis Kaylor
C/O Ariake Bible Church
488-1 Ushimizu
Arao City, Kumamoto Ken
Japan, 864-0026

LeoPhyllis@KaylorJapan.com

Ordering Information

This book is available in two formats:
- Paperback
- Hardcover

Additional copies can be purchased from:
- *XulonPress.com*
- *Amazon.com*
- Your local bookstore

Bookstores and retailers can order directly from:
- Xulon Press
- Ingram Book Company
- Spring Arbor Book Distributors